The Social Worker in Family Situations

LIBRARY OF SOCIAL WORK

GENERAL EDITOR: NOEL TIMMS
Professor of Social Work Studies
University of Newcastle upon Tyne

The Social Worker in Family Situations

William Jordan

Department of Sociology
University of Exeter

LONDON, BOSTON AND HENLEY
ROUTLEDGE & KEGAN PAUL

First published 1972
by Routledge & Kegan Paul Ltd.,
39 Store Street
London WC1E 7DD,
Broadway House, Newtown Road
Henley-on-Thames
Oxon, RG9 1EN and
9 Park Street
Boston, Mass. 02108, U.S.A.

Reprinted 1976 and 1980
Printed in Great Britain by
Redwood Burn Limited
Trowbridge & Esher

ISBN 0 7100 7266 x (c)
ISBN 0 7100 7300 3 (p)

General editor's introduction

The Library of Social Work is designed to meet the needs of students following courses of training for social work. In recent years the number and kinds of training have increased in an unprecedented way. The Library will consist of short texts designed to introduce the student to the main features of each topic of enquiry, to the significant theoretical contributions so far made to its understanding, and to some of the outstanding problems. Each volume will suggest ways in which the student might continue his work by further reading.

This book consists of the author's own case material presented in the framework of a number of interconnected arguments about social work with families. As the author notes, the movement towards such a conception of social work has recently been considerably accelerated in Britain. Social workers, looking for theories and models on which to work, may be attracted to theories about communication in families recently developed in America. William Jordan examines these and the model of family therapy they suppose and finds them wanting. He suggests that social workers are more often than not called on to deal with what he terms 'centrifugal' as opposed to the 'integrative' families who feature in the communication theories. Such families make special demands on the social worker both in terms of action and also of understanding. In the words of the author, 'unless we see the family in its social context any analysis we make of its emotional dynamics can only be misleading and incomplete.' Finally, William Jordan is concerned with the current debate within social work about the relative merits of casework and community work. The casework he describes and advocates has both width and depth and necessitates no kind of struggle to the death between casework and community work.

Like William Jordan's other book in the Library of Social Work (*Client-Worker Transactions*), this is a study informed throughout by the extensive and sensitive use of case material from the author's own practice. This is somewhat rare in British social work publications. Obviously, many questions can be raised about this approach, but its more extensive and critical use would do much to enrich social work writing and activity. We need to give to the ideas and insights which we can gain in practice the kind of treatment William Jordan offers. But this book does more than illustrate an approach; it also helps to explore from the perspective of practice the important concept of the family. We cannot expect to find within the confines of one small book 'all social workers need to know about the family', but the view-point here presented opens up a series of important questions concerning social work with the family.

NOEL TIMMS

Contents

1

Family interaction
and family casework

'Our conception of an effective family service assumes the provision of general family guidance in much of the day-to-day work of the social service departments.'[1] The Seebohm Committee was able to make this assumption because the people who gave evidence to it were more or less agreed that social workers should work with families. The arguments behind this consensus, though not stated in the Seebohm Report, were fairly straightforward. Social problems are about the way people behave towards each other; people usually live in families; therefore most social problems are also family problems. Furthermore, it is in families that people learn to behave the way they do, so the immediate causes as well as the immediate effects of their behaviour are likely to be found within their families.

In many ways, the movement towards 'family case-work' (or rather the return to popularity of this Victorian concept) grew out of a spontaneous reaction in this country against the narrow definition of the social worker's role in terms of a particular social problem or symptom, which often seemed misleadingly to nominate one member of the family as the client. This movement was given statutory encouragement by the Mental Health Act of 1959 and the Children and Young Persons Acts of 1963 and 1969, all of which encouraged work with families aimed at preventing one or more of their members having to enter institutions. These legislative developments, and the administrative changes to which they gave rise, followed a lead given by social work practice in several areas, but tended to go ahead of any developments in the same direction in the theoretical basis of social work. Family casework sprang into existence before much had been written about how to do it, and while the standard books were still analysing the casework relationship in terms of the social worker and his individual client.

The reorganisation of social work agencies under the Seebohm Report's recommendations carries the administrative trend towards family casework still further, and a good deal of the anxiety among social workers about these changes centres around the uncertain basis for family work. A further complicating factor has been that the impetus towards family work has to some extent been overtaken by the drive towards community work. For many people, the exciting part of Seebohm's proposals has been the implication that a social work department should seek to serve its whole community, and not just those individuals and families that present themselves as in need; that it should try to develop positive forces of social health, rather than a patchwork of remedies for social breakdown; that it should foster organisation in the community rather than simply dealing with disorganisation; and that it should encourage the strong to participate in its work and lend their strength to the weak, as well as allowing the weak to depend on the department itself. Thus, the idea of a community preventive service follows so closely on that of a family preventive service that the latter has hardly had time to be born. With such a strong and apparently rival force to compete with, it is natural that those who are concerned with the family approach should look around for a firm theoretical basis for family casework.

Almost simultaneously with the trend towards family casework in Britain, came a movement in American psychiatric practice which has had a similar direction, and which has given rise to a large theoretical literature. From

2

the exploration of the relationship between mental illness and the patterns of communication in the patient's family have developed theories about the contribution of family interaction to disturbed behaviour. These have an obvious appeal to family caseworkers whose task appears in many ways similar to the one undertaken by American therapists of this school.

Theories about communication in families

The concept of the 'double-bind' was the first step in the development of these theories, and it gave an apparently precise description of a pattern of communication and its effects.

> The necessary ingredients for a double-bind situation, as we see it, are: (1) Two or more people ... (2) Repeated experience ... (3) A primary negative injunction ... (4) A secondary injunction conflicting with the first at a more abstract level, and like the first enforced by punishments and signals which threaten survival ... (5) A tertiary negative injunction prohibiting escape from the field ... (6) Finally, the complete set of ingredients is no longer necessary when the victim has learned to perceive his universe in double-bind patterns.

Seen from the victim's point of view:

> The general characteristics of this situation are as follows: (1) When an individual is involved in an intense relationship; that is, a relationship in which he feels it is vitally important that he discriminate accurately what sort of message is being communicated, so that he may respond appropriately. (2) And the individual is caught in a situation in which the other person is expressing two orders of message and one of these denies the other. (3) And, the individual is unable to comment on the messages being expressed to correct his discrimination of what order to respond to ...

The authors suggested that schizophrenia occurs in a per-

3

son who has been exposed in childhood to repeated and unrelenting 'double-binds'.[2]

The original concept of the double-bind has been criticised from a number of points of view, and its very definition has proved problematical. Schuham has drawn attention to several inconsistencies between the various versions of the double-bind which have been put forward.[3] The main problem has been to define the difference in the 'levels' of communication of the two conflicting messages. Was the second message simply more abstract, as Bateson *et al.* suggested, or was it a non-verbal communication, or a meta-communication? The first definition provided an apparently simple and easily identified model of the double-bind; yet in a study carried out by Ringuette and Kennedy,[4] a panel of three people closely involved in the formulation of the double-bind hypothesis failed to agree significantly in their identification of double-binds in a series of letters written by the parents of schizophrenics and non-schizophrenics to their sons and daughters in hospitals. This would suggest that if double-binds are an identifiable phenomenon at all, the two contradictory messages must not to be communicated by the same 'channel'.

However, the problem of definition becomes even more difficult once non-verbal forms of communication are introduced. Are facial expressions, physical gestures and tone of voice all to be included? What if these are all inconsistent with each other (e.g. 'Come here', said with an angry expression, with a gesture of indifference, in a cold voice)? In spite of these difficulties, writers of the communications theory school seem to have been determined to discover some form of double-bind in every pattern of family interaction which they wish to relate to disturbed behaviour. Thus Ferreira[5] describes a family in which all the father's rules for disciplining his delinquent son are subtly contradicted by the mother. This he describes as a 'bipolar message' or 'split double-bind', because the contradictory communications took the form of a message by the father, adversely commented on by the mother. In fact, the same

4

phenomenon has long been linked with delinquency under the more old-fashioned description of inconsistency in parental discipline.

What the double-bind concept has succeeded in doing is focusing attention on the communication patterns in families, and on the possibility that contradictory communications by parents to their children could have destructive and disorganising effects. Although no connections between the double-bind phenomenon and schizophrenia could be firmly established, studies of the families of schizophrenic patients produced other theories about their patterns of relationships. These made less attempt at precise definition of forms of communication and their effects, but stressed the emotional content of the interaction, with particular reference to the child's difficulties in establishing a satisfactory individual identity. Such families were used as the basis for a concept of family homeostasis,[6] a concept of pseudomutuality[7] and a concept of need-complementarity.[8] All these theoretical contributions to the subject of family interaction were based on the specific case of the family with a schizophrenic member.

If these theories do come to be accepted as a framework for the practice of family casework it will be slightly ironical, since in many ways the movement to work with families sprang from a rejection of the psychotherapeutic, and more specifically psychoanalytic, concepts which advocated one-to-one work with individual clients. Although communications theory is concerned with family interaction rather than individual psychological mechanisms, it is none the less primarily a theory of mental illness, and is therefore in some respects open to the same criticism as its predecessor as a theoretical basis for social work. Like psychoanalytic theory, communications theory is an attempt to generalise from the phenomena alleged to give rise to a certain form of mental illness (in this case, schizophrenia, whereas Freud started from neurosis) providing a model of emotional dynamics which can in turn be applied to any other form of irrational or disturbed behaviour.

In this book I shall argue that communications theory is a misleading model for much family casework, because the concepts derived from the study of families of schizophrenics can only be misleadingly applied to the study of families with many other social problems. Thus, for instance, Ferreira notes[9] that in what he calls the 'split double-bind' in the family with a delinquent son, Bateson's 'tertiary negative injunction' did not apply.

> To the contrary, in delinquency we find that the concatenation of bipolar messages of different logical types that characterise the split double-bind often 'pushes' the victim out of the field. In certain cases that is perhaps the only stable solution for the emotional problem that they pose. In fact, it has frequently been observed that some delinquent behaviour transparently expresses an escape mechanism whose ultimate goal may be the leaving of the field.

It would appear that a double-bind which has this effect is no 'bind' at all. The point about Bateson's 'tertiary negative injunction' as a necessary condition for the double-bind was the creation of a special kind of relationship between the binder and the victim, elsewhere described as one of 'pseudomutuality' or 'need-complementarity'. Important contributory factors to the creation of such a relationship, leading ultimately to schizophrenia in the victim, are the parents' unconscious possessive needs for the child, and the social isolation of the family. In Ferreira's example, there is strong evidence that the parents used their son to fight with each other, but this is something quite different. They do not isolate him and they are not possessive of him. In this sense, although he is subject to contradictory demands, he is not bound or tied to them at all. Indeed, their communication with him might more aptly be described as a 'double catapult'.

Ferreira's example of the delinquent boy's family is familiar to social workers. The family that pushes its ado-

lescent members out before they are ready to be independent, that sees safety in separation rather than in close
and mutual relationships, that finds it easier to express
anger than affection, is readily recognised by those who
work with social problems other than mental illness. We
clearly need some theoretical concepts to help to explain
the patterns of interaction in such families, and the way
they communicate. But there is a certain *prima facie*
unlikeliness about theories which start from a model of
exaggerated mutual dependence, and seek to explain disturbed behaviour in terms of the powerful emotional ties
between family members.

The role of the therapist in communications theories

There is another important respect in which much of this
American literature appears to be inappropriate for British
social work practice. This is in the way the role of the
therapist is analysed. There is a certain beguiling simplicity,
almost amounting to naïvety, in some of their descriptions
of the therapist's role. If mental illness is the result of
contradictory or mystifying communication in the family,
the therapist's job is to untangle, unravel, and make clear.
Satir suggests[10] that ...

> the best way he can see himself is as a *resource person*
> ... The therapist does have the special advantage of
> being able to study the patient's family situation as an
> experienced observer, while remaining outside it, above
> the power struggle, so to speak. Like a camera with a
> wide-angle lens, he can see things from the position of
> each person present and act as a representative of each.
> He sees transactions, as well as the individuals involved,
> and thus has a unique viewpoint. Because of this, the
> family can place their trust in him as an 'unofficial
> observer', one who can report impartially on what he
> sees or hears. Above all, he can report on what the
> family cannot see and cannot report on. The therapist
> must also see himself as a *model of communication*.

7

Similarly, Ackerman says,[11]

> The therapist moves immediately into the life space of
> the family's current struggle ... He is taken into the fold
> as an older relative, perhaps as a grandparent endowed
> with some special wisdom concerning the problems of
> family living. He is observer, participant, supporter, acti-
> vator, challenger and reintegrator of family processes.

Case example   It is worth comparing these statements of
the therapist's role with the following short account of
my first meeting with the Painter family, one which will
I am sure be recognised sympathetically by most social
workers.

Michael Painter (aged eighteen) got into trouble with
the police for a series of minor delinquencies. When I wrote
to him before the court case, asking if I could call to see
him and his family, Michael rang to say this would not
be convenient, but he would be happy to see me at my
office. When he came in he was a cheerful, extrovert sort
of boy, without much remorse about his offences, which he
had committed with two of his friends. He was very loyal
to his friends, whose company he much enjoyed; he implied he had enjoyed the offences as well.

Michael told me that his parents had separated when he
was five years old and he had stayed with his father,
who had remarried four years later. There had been three
children of this marriage. Michael seemed to resent his
stepmother in a vague way. When I asked him about this,
it appeared that for a long time she and his father used
to go out together almost every evening, leaving him to
babysit for the family. This he resented, though recently
she had stopped going out and he had started to go out
every evening himself (in the course of which he had got
into this trouble). He vaguely felt that his stepmother was
more concerned about the other children than himself,
and that life was better when he and his father were on
their own, but he said he had never expressed any such
resentment to her or his father. I was unable to get a
strong impression of what their family life was like, or of

8

the personalities of the parents, from what Michael said, and he was obviously uncomfortable in discussing his feelings.

Next time I saw Michael, again in my office, I discussed with him the possibility of going to see him at home and meeting his family. He said straight away that his step-mother did not want me to visit the home, and she did not see why I should want to see her. I said I would like to discuss this with her, and arranged with Michael that I would contact her to do this. Michael then went on to tell me that the previous evening he had been out late, and had had to climb into his house through a window, having been locked out. His father had been furious, and had threatened to call the police.

About half an hour after Michael left the office, while I was talking to another client, the telephone rang; Mrs Painter wanted to talk to me. She angrily demanded why I should want to see her. I explained that it was normal for me to meet the parents of boys of Michael's age who were under supervision. She told me that she had been very upset about Michael getting into trouble, and also about the incident the previous evening. I said that these were matters I would like to discuss with her. Mrs Painter said she wanted to make it clear that she came from a very respectable family and she did not feel that it would be appropriate to speak to someone like me. She could not possibly have me in the home, because her three children were sensitive and intelligent and might under-stand what was happening. Of course she loved Michael too, but he was different. If I came to the home she would have no alternative but to turn Michael out. I still per-sisted in saying I wanted to meet her, and suggested that we might initially meet at my office. She said she was willing to do this, but her husband was a very different sort of person, who had been in the services, and regarded corporal punishment as the answer to everything. She implied that he would have nothing to say to me, but I said I would equally like to hear his views and discuss

9

them with him. She then handed the phone to her husband, who meekly agreed to come in to see me with Mrs Painter the following week.

About half an hour later I was still interviewing a client, with another waiting downstairs, when I heard a noise on the landing, and on opening the door found a middle-aged couple who introduced themselves as Mr and Mrs Painter. Mrs Painter did the talking. She said she wanted to see me immediately. I pointed out that there was someone with an appointment waiting, but that I would be willing to see her and her husband after seeing him, and invited them to take a seat in the waiting room. Mrs Painter said she would see me straight away or not at all, and if I would not see her then, she would throw Michael out on the street. I wished Mrs Painter good evening and started to return into my room to my waiting client. Mrs Painter stormed downstairs, with her husband in tow, saying angrily that she would put Michael out in the street at once, and that within half an hour he would be in my office, and be my responsibility.

The point about this incident is not just that the Painter family did not accept me as endowed with 'special wisdom concerning the problems of family living' or even as an 'unofficial observer'. It is rather that they seemed to be making a very definite kind of use of my intervention for their own purposes, actively turning it to their use. Not only was I not seen as an impartial expert, I was instead perceived as a means of the family getting rid of the difficult and troublesome task of coping with Michael. My intervention was rejected, but also used as an excuse for throwing Michael out. My interest in the family was taken as interference, but used as if my concern was only for Michael, and this conveniently relieved the family of their responsibility in this direction. (In fact, Michael did not turn up that evening, and two years later is still living at home. However, this does not seem to invalidate my point about how the family saw me.)

There is nothing in Satir's or Ackerman's account of

the therapist's role to prepare a social worker for this kind of pressure. They say nothing about the kind of emotional complexities which Freud, in his theory of transference and counter-transference, introduced into his account of the analytic relationship. His point was that the patient was not only tangled up in his own fantasies, but also to some extent entangled the analyst. I have suggested elsewhere[12] that the family group, in a similar way, involves the social worker in its emotional dynamics, and gives him a role to suit its purposes.

Emotional transactions between the family and the social worker

In order to understand this process, one of the most important patterns of interaction is that by which individual members of the family, or the family group as a whole, are able to put feelings which are very difficult or intolerable for them outside themselves and into one another, or into an outsider, such as a social worker. Whereas in the 'symbiotic' relationships described by Boszormenyi-Nagy, security for both parent and child lies in the closest possible relationship of mutual dependence, other families seek safety by denying the emotional content of their relationships. Where particular feelings are aroused by the family situation, but are too threatening to be expressed within the family group, these may be 'transmitted' to a social worker by an unconscious process of interaction (comparable with the transference and counter-transference phenomenon in psychoanalysis). When a social worker picks up such denied feelings in his early encounters with a family, they exert a very strong pressure on him to act in a certain way which is consistent with what the family feel to be their needs, particularly their needs for some kind of security. Thus, the family involve the social worker in a defensive manoeuvre, designed to protect the emotional *status quo* in their group, and by means of an emotional transaction provide him with a role which ensures their safety from the feelings they most fear.

It is, of course, possible for a social worker to ensure against involvement in the emotional dynamics of a family to some extent. For instance, a social worker can structure his work in a way which makes it difficult for the family to do anything but communicate with each other, and have its communications analysed. Satir gives an account of such a method. When a mother comes to the agency to complain about her teenage son's behaviour, she is told this is not how they work there. She must bring her husband, her son and her daughter. When they all come they are asked questions about the family structure and about how they communicate with each other. In particular, they are asked how they communicate their crystal-clear value messages. The family is thus persuaded to think of its difficulties in terms of its communication patterns, and no doubt some families are prepared to do this, and find it helpful. (In an article on their approach, Jackson, Satir and Riskin note that most of the families they work with are middle class.)[13]

Social work in this country is not organised in a way that would permit this approach. Departments have statutory responsibility to deal with certain social problems which arise in families, including the investigation of ill-treatment of children and the prevention of homelessness. They cannot adopt a method of working which is almost certain to be unacceptable to a majority of those referred to them, and likely to be irrelevant to the social problems of quite a few of these. They cannot turn away people who do not see the point of family therapy. This gives people who approach an agency in this country the advantage (which perhaps they deserve) of being able to present their social problems in their own terms. It takes away from the worker the power to redefine the problem completely in his terms. If the worker has to recognise the client's right to define his own social problem, then he has to lay himself open to the possibility of getting involved in

12

the emotional dynamics of the family, of being given a role which, though it suits the family for him to play it, is not necessarily the sort of role he feels he should be playing.

For this reason, the reassuring image of the family caseworker which it is possible to build upon the descriptions of the American family therapist's role is likely to be misleading. Like the reassuring image of the individual caseworker which it is still possible to find reflected in most textbooks, this is built on the myth that the worker is in control, understands what is going on better than the clients do, is capable of rational, objective diagnosis and planning, has skills and a choice of methods of work available to him. This myth helps to protect the worker from the painful reality of a job in which he is frequently cast defenceless into emotional relationships with difficult people who often have a keen intuitive sense of what is going on and a very considerable and alarming ability to make disastrous things happen. It seems to me more profitable to look at the reality of the family caseworker's position—painful, uncertain, vulnerable—without the protection of a reassuring theory.

What then is the reality that confronts a social worker about to try and work with a family? In fact, he is simply one person facing a group of other people, who share a common life together, with shared values and shared patterns of behaviour. He is working on behalf of an established authority that they at best distrust, at worst detest. His own cultural and class background is usually very different from that of the family, and they are likely to be well aware of this discrepancy. Thus, they are usually aware that their shared family norms, which are the basis of their life together, are not the same as his norms about family life, and this is likely to put them on the defensive.

Family norms and interaction

Norms of family life tend to be unspecific, as Bott found in her study of family and social relationships.[14] She discovered that her respondents had difficulty in making such norms explicit at all, and that they found it easier to describe the norms governing their other roles, such as those at work. This must be partly because patterns of family life are not rigidly defined by a set of rules, but gradually evolved as a result of the delicate emotional balance between the needs of each of the members of the family. Such norms represent the sum total of all the years of conflict, compromise and concern for each other through which the family have built up all they have in the way of happiness, security and mutual support, and protected themselves against the potential miseries and uncertainties of life together. Although, as Leichter and Mitchell have shown,[15] there is much scope for confusion and misunderstanding between clients and social workers over such questions as the closeness of relationships with wider kinship networks, the area of clients' greatest defensiveness is likely to concern the immediate relationships within the nuclear family group. The experience of having someone coming to make a critical assessment of family life according to a set of unfamiliar criteria must be recognisable for anyone with children who has been called on by a Health Visitor. Yet at least in this example the aspects of family life which are open to criticism are fairly marginal. It is possible to clean up the place a bit without necessarily having a very deep effect on the day-to-day quality of life. The defensiveness would be very much deeper if it was felt that what was being assessed, and what might possibly require change, was the emotional substance of the family's patterns of getting on together.

Thus, if a family has a social problem, such as the delinquency or mental illness of one of its children, which it may well have been trying to conceal or deal with itself for several years, this problem, with all the difficulties it may have caused the family, may well seem much less frightening in its consequences than the overthrow of the whole balance of emotional forces which the family has achieved. Suppose, for instance, the mother in the family had a history of mental instability before she met her husband. Such a secret, with all the fears it generates, is likely to get buried very deep in the family's consciousness, and yet to have a subtle and all-pervading effect on the quality of their interaction. The father who knows about it will pattern his behaviour towards his wife in a way that takes account of her vulnerability, both helping her to suppress and deny it, yet indicating in his moods and actions, especially in a crisis, his fear of the danger it represents. This fear may well be communicated to the children, so that they react in accord with their father, without quite knowing why. After all, the mother's stability is essential to family life, and her breakdown would be the greatest possible threat to it. Thus in every crisis or conflict, the mother is protected from the full force of the emotional pressures within herself. She may well be helped to deny her weakness or her destructive anger, even at the expense of another member of the family, who acts it out on her behalf. A delinquent or disturbed child, seen from the outside as the 'victim' of the family's interaction, may from the inside be sensed in some way to be saving the family from the total destruction that would take place if the central figure was forced to carry all her feelings.

So a social worker who comes into the family to look for the emotional origins of a social problem can represent a potentially dangerous and destructive force where the pattern of family interaction is designed to fulfil this protective function. The family as a whole, without necessarily being aware of quite what it is doing or why, will mount a defensive manoeuvre against the danger of change and the threat it represents. In the example I gave of the Painter family, Mrs Painter struck me as a very unstable woman, who was possibly mentally ill. But for the family, even for Michael, her stability and theirs seemed to depend on first repelling any attempt on my part to upset the family's equilibrium, and secondly inducing me to take responsibility for the difficult Michael.

If a social worker fails to take account of the strong forces in families by which they defend themselves against change, and also of the very strong fears upon which such defensive manoeuvres are based, he is likely to over-estimate his potential as an agent for changing patterns of interaction, and be repeatedly disappointed in his dealing with families. This is particularly true of work with families which have established, perhaps over several generations, patterns of interaction which they regard as normal, and upon which they feel their security rests, but which involve a type of behaviour by one or more members which is considered unacceptable by the rest of society. The extreme case is of a pattern where the family rely on the social worker to play a part which they feel is essential to the survival of the family, but which he feels is contrary to the aims and functions of his agency. An example of this is to be found in those families which, by their past experience or through the parents' early upbringing, have come to depend on one member being admitted to a kind of institution (hospital, approved school, etc.) to which the social worker to some extent controls access. Whereas the worker may regard this kind of action as precisely what he is trying to prevent, the family may see it as the only possible means of ensuring that it does not disintegrate completely (see chapter 3).

Social and economic factors in family interaction

It is this kind of family that demonstrates most vividly the fact that many families do not share the norms of social functioning, based on norms of family living, which are represented by the agency's function, and in which the worker thus has an official interest. Some families have come to expect such events as the short-term reception of children into care, or temporary separations through homelessness, as part of the pattern of life; some have even come to rely on them as means of achieving some kind of continuity, where the alternative would be a more permanent breaking of the group. The expectation that a family should be self-sufficient and provide for itself in every possible circumstance is based on the norms of the comfortably-off members of society. It is one thing to say that such norms create stability and minimise social disorganisation; but the norms of these other families, though apparently disruptive and damaging for themselves, may well represent an adaptation to external circumstances which are highly disorganising and destructive of family life, and to which, as a result of their experience of poverty or bad housing, they have become accustomed.

One of the difficulties of the notion of 'functional' and 'dysfunctional' families which Satir puts forward[16] is precisely this difference in the material circumstances in which families in different social classes live. The distinction is based purely on the patterns of communication in the family group, and is supposed to differentiate between families which are mentally healthy and those which are mentally unhealthy for their members. On the face of it, it seems unlikely that an objective definition of 'functional' communications patterns can be reached which will apply equally to a well-to-do family living in a London suburb and to a gipsy family in a caravan. However clearly the gipsy family may communicate, they are going to have certain problems of family living which the suburban family do not. These problems (such as overcrowding, the necessity for frequent moves, and social isolation) are likely to cause the family to develop patterns of interaction which are particularly suited to their situation, but which are quite different from those of the family living in the suburbs. We would therefore need different criteria to judge whether a gipsy family's interaction was 'functional' from the standards we would use to evaluate the interaction of the suburban family.

Furthermore, the very way of life of the gipsy family,

which is determined by its economic and social position in the community, may be seen by other more influential groups as constituting a social problem. For instance, a social worker may find himself working with a gipsy family whose 'homelessness' consists in a refusal by the local authority to allow the family to stay in the area where they have been living. The communications theory approach to family social problems is thus open to the objection that it fails to allow for the possibility of social problems that arise entirely out of environmental circumstances such as these. But even where there are other problems (such as delinquency amongst the children of the gipsy family) which could be related to the emotional quality of family life, the 'dysfunctional' approach seems to give families too little credit for being the experts at living their own lives in the particular circumstances which have been imposed upon them. Social workers would seem to be well advised to take further account of environmental and cultural factors in assessing a family's pattern of interaction than the communications theory would encourage them to do.

Some radical social workers are coming to doubt the extent to which a middle-class expert in human relations can help a family living in poverty and bad housing in an urban environment which offers them little escape from the worst that society has to offer, whether in education, recreation, cultural amenities or employment opportunities. These critics of the present structure of social work point out that much of what goes on appears to represent the imposition by social workers of the norms of social and family life of the dominant classes upon disadvantaged groups. This activity is seen as aimed at providing a substitute for the material and environmental needs of these groups, while simultaneously controlling the more disruptive elements within them.

If social work is to be really concerned with the quality of family life, then it must show its concern with these material and environmental problems more tangibly. There is some hope that with the reorganisation of social work agencies under the Seebohm proposals, some authorities will begin to do this. The danger is that this kind of work will be allotted to specialists (perhaps called community workers) and that work with individuals and families with other identifiable social problems will continue to be done by caseworkers. While casework has always paid lip-service to the contribution made by material and environmental factors to the problems of its clients, its real concern, in recent years especially, has been with emotional factors. If it adopts American communications theory as the basis for family casework, this will be another step in the same direction.

This might well cause a split in social work between casework, which deals with social problems as if they were emotional in origin, and community work, concerned with material and environmental problems. In the long run it could even result in two halves of the same social work agency apparently working against each other, the case-workers for social control, and the community workers for the social and economic liberation of disadvantaged groups.

At least part of the answer to this dilemma seems to be in a much increased interest by family caseworkers in the actual patterns of family life of the kind of people who become clients. Such an interest might well reveal both cultural and emotional factors which would not be apparent from a 'functional' approach based on considerations of mental health and illness. If social workers are genuinely concerned about the social as well as the emotional content of the lives of the families with which they work, they may in fact get more rather than less insight into the emotional factors which govern patterns of family interaction. For without this interest in the total content of family life, some psychological 'insights' are likely to be simple misunderstandings. Leichter and Mitchell's study in New York found that clients rarely reported that problems with their kin had led them to seek help, but workers frequently reported that problems relating to came up in treatment. As a result, 40 per cent of sework methods adopted involved the reduction of clients' involvement with kin and particularly the loosening of ties between clients and their parents (e.g. between a wife and her mother). This approach seemed to be linked with the fact that only 14 per cent of caseworkers, as opposed to 42 per cent of clients, endorsed the statement, 'it is usually fine for a young married couple to live near their parents', while only 16 per cent of caseworkers and 65 per cent of clients thought that 'it's selfish for someone to cut himself off from his relatives'. Similar clashes between clients' norms of family life and the values arising from either the professional culture or the middle-class family background of social workers are reported by Mayer and Timms.[17]

It is unfortunate that while there has for a long time existed a considerable sociological literature about the family patterns which are associated with working-class culture, this has apparently failed to influence social workers to the same extent as the psychological study of the problems of mental health, based on a functional analysis of the nuclear family. Perhaps this is partly because the latter can provide precise models of family interaction, however unrepresentative or misleading, whereas sociological theory is necessarily more formal and less specific. What I have therefore attempted to do in this book is to describe some alternative patterns of interaction in the nuclear family to the ones which have been analysed in detail by the communications theory school, and to suggest some ways in which a social worker in family situations like these might react. The phenomena which I shall describe as family patterns are obviously linked to wider social and economic factors, and in the final chapter I shall try to make some connections between methods of work and these important considerations.

My approach has something in common with the double-bind theory, in that it is describing a pattern of family

20

interaction and linking it with behaviour by an individual member of the family which is socially disapproved. However, my purpose is not to set out another model of dysfunctional family interaction. It is rather to show that the patterns to be found in the families of people with social problems are often more linked with normal adaptations to the problems of family life which have been documented in the sociological literature of the family than they are with the 'dysfunctional' patterns of interaction which have interested those who have studied the families of schizophrenic patients.

References

1 *Report of the Committee on Local Authority and Allied Personal Social Services.* Cmnd 3703. HMSO, 1968, para. 274.
2 G. Bateson, D. D. Jackson, J. Haley and J. Weakland, 'Toward a theory of schizophrenia', *Behavioral Science,* 1956, 1, 251-64.
3 A. I. Schuham, 'The double-bind hypothesis a decade later', *Psychological Bulletin,* 1967, vol. 68 (6), 409-16.
4 E. L. Ringuette and T. Kennedy, 'An experimental study of the double-bind hypothesis', *Journal of Abnormal Psychology,* 1966, 71, 136-41.
5 A. J. Ferreira, 'The double-bind and delinquent behaviour', *Archives of General Psychiatry,* 1960, 3, 359-67.
6 D. D. Jackson, 'The question of family homeostasis', *Psychiatric Quarterly* (Supplement), 1957, 31, 79-90.
7 L. C. Wynne, I. M. Ryckoff, J. Day and S. I. Hirsch, 'Pseudomutuality in the family relations of schizophrenics', *Psychiatry,* 1958, 21, 205-20.
8 I. Boszormenyi-Nagy, 'The concept of schizophrenia from the perspective of family treatment', *Family Process,* 1962, 1, 103-13.
9 Ferreira, op. cit.
10 V. Satir, *Conjoint Family Therapy,* Science and Behavior Books Inc., 1967.
11 N. W. Ackerman, 'Family psychotherapy and psycho-

analysis: the implications of difference', *Family Process*, 1962, 1, 30-43.

12   W. J. O. Jordan, *Client-Worker Transactions*, Routledge & Kegan Paul, 1970.

13   D. D. Jackson, V. Satir and J. Riskin, 'A method of analysis of a family interview', *Archives of General Psychiatry*, 1961, 5, 321-39.

14   E. Bott, *Family and Social Network*, Tavistock, 1957.

15   H. Leichter and W. Mitchell, *Kinship and Casework*, Russel Foundation, 1967.

16   Satir, op. cit.

17   J. E. Mayer and N. Timms, *The Client Speaks: Working Class Impressions of Casework*, Routledge & Kegan Paul, 1970.

2
Centrifugal families

One criticism which could be made of the communications theory approach to family interaction is that it starts by looking at the ways family members behave towards each other without first looking at the activities which the family is trying to perform. It is hard to say what is wrong with the way a family is doing things without first asking what it is that it is trying to do. The answers to this question lie in the wider context of family relationships, and in the position of the family in society.

Sociologists have been more-or-less agreed about the functions that the family characteristically performs. Murdock[1] lists four functions; the sexual, the reproductive, the economic and the educational (including the socialisation of children). In an industrialised society, some of these functions are usually shared with other social institutions such as businesses and schools.

Sociological contributions to the understanding of family roles

But to say that the 'family' performs these functions is to say very little about the particular roles of individual members of the family in these activities. Especially in the economic and educational spheres, there are wide variations in the ways that individual members play their roles, and one important factor in determining the kind of roles played is the extent to which the family group is engaged in these activities. For instance, if a grandmother or an aunt play some part in the socialisation of children, the importance of the mother's role may be diminished, but her potential economic role is increased. If a teenage son is expected to make a financial contribution, some of the economic responsibility may be removed from the father. Studies such as Willmott and Young's[2] in East London and Rosser and Harris's[3] in Swansea show that wider kinship relationships have an important part to play in the activities of many families in these spheres. Thus, it is not only misleading to think of the nuclear family alone as performing these functions, but it is also difficult to understand the roles of the parents without knowing more about how these fit in with those of other kin, who are often involved in the day-to-day life of the family.

But it is not only relationships with kin which affect the way members of the family interact with each other. Bott[4] has pointed out that where each of the partners was involved in a close-knit network of social relationships before marriage, and these networks continue to be open for them after marriage, the availability of alternative sources of emotional satisfaction make the partners less dependent on the marital relationship. In a critical assessment of Bott's study, Harris points out that this is most likely to occur where each partner belongs to a single-sex group, whose members share norms of marital role segregation.[5] On the other hand, where the partners' networks are loose knit, mutual assistance between members will be less consistent, and the norms of the groups will be less influential on the partners' behaviour. In such circumstances, as Bott suggests, the partners will be more likely to develop a 'joint conjugal role relationship'.

In Bott's study there seemed to be important differences between the families with joint conjugal roles and those with segregated roles. In the latter the partners tended to stress the importance of relationships in the extended family, but did not think that the quality of their sexual relationship was so important. Those with joint roles were

24

more concerned with their sexual relationship and less with kin, as well as paying more attention to companionship and mutual support.

There have been several theories about the emergence of the nuclear family with a joint conjugal pattern as a self-sufficient unit. Parsons[6] has pointed out that an industrialised society demands geographical mobility in many occupations, and that it is the nuclear family that has come to be the mobile unit. Goode suggests that the independent nuclear family is likely to be characteristic of those social classes seeking upward social mobility.[7] Harris argues that both nuclear and extended family patterns co-exist in most industrialised societies because geographical mobility is not required in all occupational roles. Neither Bott nor Rosser and Harris found very large differences between family patterns in this respect on the basis of social class.

What seems to emerge, therefore, from these sociological studies of the family is a continuum from the interdependence of the isolated nuclear family at one end, to the segregated roles and close-knit social networks at the other, with the vast majority of families somewhere in the middle. But it is hard to see how anybody can hope to understand patterns of interaction in a nuclear family group without some reference to these factors. For if the roles of the marriage partners are to such an extent determined by their expectations of the behaviour of people in the wider family and social network around them, then it makes little sense to analyse these roles without taking account of the social resources available to individual members outside the family. Given that the existence of such networks indicates that the members of nuclear families need social contact and support from outside their group, it would seem that even the absence of a social network must give rise to repercussions inside the family which are likely to be as significant as those which occur through availability of such a network.

Integrative and centrifugal families

The pattern of relationships which Bateson and his followers have identified and connected with schizophrenia has been analysed in terms of its emotional origins and consequences in the nuclear family group. But the tendency of family members to bind each other together, in a sometimes confusing and mystifying way, to the exclusion of the outside world, must also be related in some way to these social factors external to the nuclear family. Furthermore, this tendency towards very close emotional ties represents only one extreme in a continuum, at the opposite end of which are those families in which members seek to escape from all involvement with each other by fleeing from the family into the outside world. This is a tendency which is often very strongly illustrated in the families of people with some social problems other than mental illness. It is worth trying to relate these 'emotional' patterns to the broader patterns of the family's social interaction.

The origins of both emotional patterns seem to lie in a conflict between those needs and aspirations which draw family members together for mutual help and support and the needs and aspirations which drive individual members into the outside world. This conflict can perhaps best be seen in families containing adolescent children, whose emotional and social needs are both very great, and who are trying to learn to satisfy needs outside the family at a time when their need for emotional support from their parents is still very strong. From the examples given by Laing and Esterson,[8] it seems that in families of schizophrenics the emotional ties are so strong that the parents cannot let their children go, and often try instead to create their own self-sufficient social system within the family membership. The opposite tendency is found in certain families in which the emotional content of family life is habitually denied or played down, and members seek to satisfy all their emotional needs in social activities away

26

from the home. For such families, emotional crises are seen as best dealt with by bursts of activity in some sphere outside the family's group activities, and social problems and their solutions are usually thought of in environmental and material terms.

The families described by Laing and Esterson embody, in an extreme form, the notion that family life should provide the emotional basis for the lives of each of its participants, and that it is in the family that emotional needs should be met. The parents of schizophrenics often said of their children such things as: 'She's always been with me, I took her with me, I never left her.' They felt that it was important for parents and children to 'get on well together' and for there to be no 'disharmony'. In describing how she wanted her relationship with her daughter to be, one mother said she wished to be 'at one with her'.

It is instructive to contrast this pattern with the one Harris gives[9] of family life in a 'small, rather old-fashioned segment' of the working class, in a neighbourhood where the work is unusually heavy manual labour, wages are relatively low and housing standards poor. This picture is created by 'drawing together elements from a number of British studies dealing with a certain type of working class family life'.

Marriage is seen as an arrangement whereby a man obtains sexual and domestic services from a woman in return for economic provision. Large family size and poor domestic conditions on the one hand, and long hours of work on the other, preclude joint activities of husband and wife outside the domestic sphere, and limit co-operation within it. The women ... are dependent on what help they can get from each other ... Hence little is expected of marriage, and the criteria that are applied in evaluating a husband are that he should be a good provider, not knock the kids about, not spend too much time or money drinking with his mates, and not 'bother you', while a good wife is a 'good manager', who lets you 'bother her', always has a hot meal ready

27

> when you come home, generally organises the house-
> hold to suit your convenience and doesn't nag.

It is clear from this description of family life that it is not part of the expectation of family members that their emotional needs should be met to any great extent in the family group. Instead, they expect their emotional as well as their social needs to be met in their separate networks of extended family and social relationships; the husband in the work and peer group that 'dominates the whole social life of the men', the wife among her female neighbours and relations.

If we now turn to the examples that Laing and Esterson give of parents with schizophrenic daughters, it is possible to see how close family ties and emotional interdependence do not abolish the social needs of family members, but may instead lead to their expression within the family group.

Three characteristics of Laing and Esterson's families stand out from the interviews they present. In the first place, these family groups are isolated from the rest of the world. Second, the parents cling to their daughters, allowing them no autonomy, treating them as part of themselves, and denying them any social life outside the family. Third, the parents create a form of social life for themselves within the family, using their relationships with their children to compensate them for their isolation. It is worth looking at their examples in more detail to see some of the patterns of interaction which both reflect and perpetuate these characteristics.

The isolation of these families from the rest of the world was often the result of the parents' fears about other people. Lucie Blair's parents were afraid for different reasons. For Mr Blair, men were all alike, and 'none could be trusted'. For Mrs Blair 'everyone knew everyone else's business, or wanted to ... It was best to keep to oneself and never tell anyone "your business".' Claire Church's parents attributed to her fears of crowds and of men (which she denied) which were clearly their own. 'Mrs

Church was terrified of "crowds", especially those small "crowds" (in ordinary language, a party) where sexual and other possibilities arise—small parties where people drink, let their hair down, and are a little more spontaneous than usual for a short while.' Mrs King, since her marriage, 'has hardly ever been outside the house unaccompanied by her own mother or father, apart from visits to the local shops. She has extensive fears of travelling, of meeting people. Her self-consciousness amounts to ideas that people look at her in the street, and that they are making ridiculous remarks about her.'

These fears of the parents, and their resultant isolation, provide part of the explanation of why they need to bind their daughters to themselves. Maya Abbott's parents saw any attempt by her to gain autonomy or a separate identity as 'illness', 'since it entailed that she did not "fit in" with them'. Lucie Blair's life was rigidly defined by her father:

> His daughter was made to be a gentlewoman. There had always been a place for her at home. With a generous sweep of his arm he said that he did not object to her leaving the house. She could go down to the local shops any time she wished. Going out alone at night was, of course, another matter. He expressed to us that the dangers were of being kidnapped or raped. He definitely disapproved of her entering a cinema alone, and was very doubtful about her visiting a theatre.

Claire Church was told by her parents that she was afraid of other people and felt herself that she hadn't 'really been encouraged tremendously to mix with other people'. Mrs Church 'was very concerned about the dangers that might befall Claire at the hands of people in particular social gatherings, especially sexual dangers.' When asked, 'What do you perceive as being wrong with June this weekend?', Mrs Field answered, 'Well, on Saturday for instance, June wanted to go to the Youth Club ...' Mrs Head insisted that her daughter Jean never wanted to go

to the cinema, to go out with boys outside her own deno-
mination, to have sexual relations before marriage, to go
to dances or restaurants. Jean said she wanted to and did,
even though her parents had tried to govern her life in
all important respects. Mrs King never allowed Hazel to
go out alone with her father. 'The extent to which Hazel
was kept within a set of relations comprising her mother,
grandmother and grandfather was remarkable. Even relations with her younger brothers and with her father were
forbidden or discouraged.'

In order to make up in some part for the impoverish-
ment of their social lives, these parents attempted to provide their daughters, and to get their daughters to provide
for them, some of the satisfactions that would normally be
sought by all members outside the family group. Maya
Abbott's parents expected her to confide in them about
everything she thought and felt, to tell them about everything she did. Claire Church said her mother, who at
one time had been in business until she gave this up
through ill-health, 'is more of a managing director than a
mother. She was more interested in business than in being
a mother and she brought the business-woman's attitude
into the home.' Although Mrs Church was very afraid
of 'crowds', and saw everyone outside the family as
menacing, family life itself was institutionalised, and con-
ducted 'in a tone and manner that suggests that she is
giving a report to a board meeting'. Sarah Danzig had
given up all attempt at relationships with people outside
the family, and had withdrawn to a bed-ridden existence.
Her father, who was 'secretly sexually dissatisfied', criticised her for this, even though she gave as a reason for
her withdrawal that her father had given her no privacy
at all. Her father said, 'Well, one of the reasons why I
personally was interested in her social life is not because
I was prying into her private affairs; I was mainly interested in watching that she shouldn't be impressed by funny
stories'. His activities included 'unannounced intrusions
into her bedroom when she was undressed, unsolicited

insistence on tidying up her bedroom, listening in on her telephone calls, intercepting her letters, and so on.... All such behaviour was either denied by him or rationalised as out of love for her.'

Their daughters' 'illnesses' drew these families still closer together, and provided yet another emotional focus within the family. In every case their reaction to the 'illness' was to try to integrate the daughter still further into the life of the family, to make her more part of themselves, to create more family harmony, to get on better together, to try to understand her more, where 'understanding' meant trying to get her to think in their way. In contrast, what I shall call 'centrifugal' families presuppose that it is only away from family life that emotional satisfactions can be obtained, and that personal needs, whether emotional or social, can be met.

It is worth comparing the kind of pattern of family life reflected in these examples from Laing and Esterson with that which is to be found in the families of many delinquent boys.[10] I shall suggest from examples from my own experience that such families follow a pattern which is diametrically opposite to the families of schizophrenics. Whereas the schizophrenic girls were isolated from their peers, the delinquent boys (and the other teenage members of their family) are usually involved in an extremely full social life. They are very active members of a peer group (often a gang) but usually also have girl friends to provide them with another whole set of social activities, often quite different from the peer group ones. They also have social contacts through work which frequently provide another network of acquaintances and of activities. The parents of these boys are usually involved in many more contacts and activities outside the home during their leisure hours than the parents of the schizophrenic girls. However, they frequently unfavourably contrast the range of their activities and outlets with those of their children, and complain that unlike the teenagers they are 'tied' to the family, that their responsibilities will not allow them to lead as full a life as they would like. They tend to remember the time before they were married, or before they had children, as a golden age. They express dissatisfaction with the limitations of a family existence, and although they make some token effort at controlling their sons' involvement with peer groups and with girl friends, and sometimes tell them to stay in more, they are often openly envious of them, and imply in much of what they say about themselves and their children that the only way to satisfy emotional needs and be happy is to escape as much as possible from the bonds of family life.

Unlike the families of schizophrenics, which draw closer together at times of stress, and react to emotional discord in the family group by trying to create harmony and 'like thinking', centrifugal families deal with difficulties by rushing away from what they see to be their source, the emotional matrix of family life. If they cannot achieve this, because of 'duties' towards the family, then they threaten to do it. Here is an example of this process in the Horn family.

Example of a centrifugal family: the Horns

When I first got to know the Horn family they had been concerned with social workers for many years because of various social problems, mainly to do with their children. Mr Horn (aged fifty-three) and Mrs Horn (aged forty-eight) had five children and their problems with them seemed to stem from their difficulties in getting on with each other, though they themselves certainly did not see the solution to their problems in terms of an improved marital relationship. They had separated briefly on several occasions, when Mrs Horn had left her husband, taking some of the children. Mr Horn, an ex-farm labourer turned factory hand, was quick tempered and very jealous of his wife, though he showed nothing of this in his dealings with the outside world, and particularly in his relationships with people in authority, to whom he was polite and charming, being always co-operative and anxious to make a good impression. However, the whole of the rest of his family, taking their lead from Mrs Horn, seemed to isolate him and make him into a sort of ogre figure. He was certainly quick tempered, insecure and inconsistent but he seemed genuinely fond of both his wife and his children.

Mrs Horn was a tiny, bitter, sharp-tongued woman who did nothing but complain and seemed never to have a good word for anyone. She had been removed from her parents on the grounds of cruelty when she was a small child and brought up under strict discipline in an 'orphanage'. She gave an impression of having been completely deprived of affection, and everything she said was negative, making it quite clear that she did not believe in emotional relationships, or that happiness was possible in family life. She talked of the role of the wife in general terms as an unpaid servant, and her particular role as that of a misused slave to her ungrateful children and violent husband. In spite of this she never went out except on family visits, and devoted nearly all her time to work in the home and to looking after the children's material needs, which she did more than adequately on a small income. Several of them looked rather over-fed, and they were always well dressed. Mrs Horn explained this in terms of her 'duties' and 'responsibilities' but she insisted that she would be delighted to be rid of these along with the children. She described happiness entirely in terms of 'freedom' and 'getting away from all this'. She couldn't say what sort of life this would entail in practical terms, but felt that it was a right which had been denied her, first by her upbringing, and then by her marriage which she had undertaken to escape from her previous situation. She insisted that she had absolutely no love for the children, and reinforced this by saying very rejecting things in front of them and how glad she would be when they left home.

Mr and Mrs Horn had some difficulties with all their children, but two of them were by now married and had

33

left home. Still living at home were Frank (aged seventeen), Norman (aged twelve) and Julia (aged eight). The current problem was Norman. My first impression of him was more of a small wild dog than a child, the main difference being that Norman could climb trees. His first reaction to me was to run away and hide, and several of my early conversations with him were carried on from the foot of a tree into which he used to climb for refuge. He seemed totally confused and lost. When I first saw him he had been refusing to go to school for six months, and had succeeded, in spite of all the efforts of the school authorities. He was obviously very dependent on his mother, yet her real complaint about him was of his violence towards her, which was frequent and took the form of hitting her and smashing her crockery and belongings. He also quarrelled violently with his father, who tended to retaliate violently to this.

Norman's truancy presents a vivid contrast with the same behaviour as it might occur in a family such as those Laing and Esterson describe. In such families, failure to attend school is often the result of subtle pressure by the parents on the child to draw him further into the family circle and withdraw him from the school. The mother in one such family, when faced with difficulty over her son's schooling, offered to educate him herself. In another family, the father had given up work in order to devote himself to looking after his wife, who had various symptoms including an overwhelming fear of the outside world. Gradually neither parents left the house at all, and finally the child began to come home from school on various pretexts, or to fail to go in the mornings. By contrast, Norman's parents were angry and rejecting towards him about his behaviour. They threatened him that he would be 'sent away' if he did not go to school, and appeared to support the authorities in their efforts to get him there. Even though an important part of Norman's feelings about staying away from school was to do with the emotional climate of the home (he said he was afraid of fights between his parents developing, and of his mother leaving home while he was at school) he reacted against both his father and particularly his mother, fighting with them and shouting at them very often. Also, when he was not at school he did not stay at home but roamed around in the village or in the countryside, more like a wild animal than a timid child.

When I took over supervision of Norman, after he had appeared in court for truancy, I arranged for him to make a fresh start at a different school, and he said he would co-operate in this venture. However, he did not go on the first day, and fought violently with his mother in the morning. The second day I called at nine o'clock, and Norman had again refused to go and had disappeared. Mrs Horn said she was sick of fighting him, and Mr Horn offered to take responsibility for getting him ready the following morning if I was again to call at 9 a.m. (Mr Horn was on night work, and arrived home at 8 a.m.) The arrangement we made was that Mrs Horn would leave Norman in bed until she left to take the youngest child to school, when Mr Horn would get him up and ready for my arrival. The following recording (written immediately after the event) gives an impression of what happened, and the kind of interaction taking place in the Horn family in face of this difficult situation:

When I reached the house, the door was opened by Mr Horn who showed me into the kitchen, where Norman was standing in his pyjama tops and underpants.

Norman: (*shouting and crying*) 'I'm not going!'
Mr Horn: 'Get your clothes on!'
Norman: 'I'm not going! I'm not!'
Mr Horn: 'Do as you're told!'
Norman: 'I won't go!'
Mr Horn (*to W.J.*) 'It's been all I could do not to hit him.' (*Threatening gesture to Norman.*)
Norman: 'I'll kill you! Leave me alone. I'm not going.'

35

W.J.: 'Okay Mr Horn, you'd better leave him to me. Thanks for what you've done.'
(*Mr Horn goes into the front room, leaving me with Norman, crying, with his hands over his eyes. Short pause.*)

At this stage I felt I might be able to get Norman over his tantrum by talking quietly with him, helping him to face his fears, and that I might even get him to change his mind about coming to school, given enough time. It was the first chance I had had to speak to him since he had failed to go to the new school.

W.J.: (*quietly*) 'Well, what's happened since Friday to make you change your mind about going to the new school?'
Norman: 'Nothing. I'm not going.'
W.J.: 'You said you would go. What's made you change?'
Norman: 'I don't know.'
W.J.: 'I didn't really expect you to go by yourself on Monday. I knew you'd be scared. But you ran away from me yesterday.'
Norman: 'I'm not going to school.'
W.J.: 'What's happened this morning?'
Norman: 'My Dad hit me. He said he'd hit me.'
W.J.: 'But he didn't hit you. He was just trying to get you to go to school.'
Norman: 'I hate him. I'm not going.'
W.J.: 'You'd rather go back to court?'
Norman: 'I don't care.'
W.J.: 'You didn't like court last time.'
Norman: 'No.'
W.J.: 'You admitted it was worse than school.'
Norman: 'I don't care if they do send me away. I'll be glad to get out of this dump.'
W.J.: 'You want to be taken away from home?'
Norman: 'I don't care.'
W.J.: 'You don't like being with your parents?'
Norman: 'Mum's all right. I hate him.'

36

W.J.: 'He's trying to do something to stop you being sent away. Is that wrong?'

Norman: 'I don't know.'

W.J.: 'You want to get away from home, is that right?'

Norman: 'No.'

W.J.: 'What then?'

Norman: 'I'm not going to school.'

W.J.: 'I realise you're scared of going to school. I'm not trying to pretend it's nice and easy. It's just that there are worse things, and you know it.'

(*Pause.*)

W.J.: 'You don't really want to be taken away from home, do you?'

(*Pause. Norman has stopped crying and is looking thoughtful. He is almost looking at me for the first time.*)

W.J.: 'Perhaps you think I don't mean the things I say, but don't forget, I've done everything I said so far.'

(*Pause. Noise at the front door. In comes Mrs Horn, bursts straight into the kitchen, followed by Mr Horn.*)

Mrs Horn: 'Oh God, is this still going on? I've had enough, I can't take any more. I've been out of this house since ten to nine.'

Mr Horn: 'All right, dear, all right.'

Mrs Horn: 'Four kids when I got to that school, that's all there was, four bloody kids. I've had enough, I'm getting out.'

Norman: (*screaming again*) 'He hit me, Mum, he hit me!'

Mr Horn: 'I never did.'

Mrs Horn: 'He'd better not, or I'll have the police on him. I can't take any more, I'm getting out.' (*She goes to the front door.*)

Norman: 'Mum!' (*screaming*) 'Mum, come here!' (*Mrs Horn returns immediately.*)

Mrs Horn: 'I can't take any more of this.'

W.J.: 'What can't you take any more of?'

Mrs Horn: 'I've fought and fought to get him to go to school. I'm not fighting any more.'

W.J.: 'You mean he'll have to be taken away from you?'

37

Mrs Horn: 'I don't care. I'd be better off without any of them. You do the best you can for them and this is what you get. I've had enough.'

Mr Horn: 'No one could have tried harder than my missus.'

W.J.: 'So now you're saying that you want him to be taken away by the court?'

Mrs Horn: 'They can come if they like. They won't find me here. I'll take him and Julia and get out. I've done it before.'

Mr Horn: 'Now don't start that, dear.'

W.J.: 'So you do mind about him being taken away?'

Mrs Horn: 'I don't care. They none of them worry about me. The two that are married only come here when they feel like it, and the other two curse and swear at me. I'd be better off without any of them.'

W.J.: 'But you said you'd run away if they came for Norman?'

Mrs Horn: 'I've had enough. I can't stand any more of this. It all comes back to me. Even you said I think they turn against me, that they all take it out on me.'

Mr Horn: 'It's not what she thinks, they are like that. No one could have done more than her.'

W.J.: 'I never said you thought they behaved like that. I said you'd been treated like that all your life, ever since you were in the orphanage. You've come to expect people to treat you like that.'

Mrs Horn: 'I don't expect it, they just do.'

W.J.: 'Perhaps that's because you've been treated like that all along; you don't know any other way of being treated.'

Mrs Horn: 'I can't take any more of it, I know that.'

W.J.: 'You seem to be saying that I'm treating you the same way.'

Mrs Horn: 'Well, you seem to blame me. It's not my fault. I always got him to school when we lived at Ashgate. The others all went. I've fought with him, I've had enough. I'd be better off without him.'

W.J.: 'You seem to be saying I'm persecuting you now,

with what I'm doing. I'm trying to help prevent him being taken away. Is that wrong?'

Mrs Horn: 'I wish they would take him away. He's been nothing but a worry to me. I've had enough of it. He always went at Ashgate. I could get him to go more than anybody else.'

W.J.: 'You seem to be saying that if it wasn't for me and Mr Horn, you could get him to go to school.'

Mrs Horn: 'He always used to go to school, didn't he?'

Norman: 'Yes, not for him.'

W.J.: 'Are you saying, Norman, that you'd go to school for your mother now?'

Norman: 'Yes.'

W.J.: 'Okay, let's try that tomorrow then, if that's what you want. Is that what you want, Mrs Horn?'

Mrs Horn: 'I've had enough of it. He used to go.'

W.J.: 'Well, if that's the way you want it, I won't come tomorrow, and I suppose you'd better stay out of the way too, Mr Horn.'

Mr Horn: 'I've got to get to bed. I need the sleep. I'll have to come home.'

W.J.: 'Well, I take it that Norman will be catching the ten to eight bus, so you only have to come home a bit later.'

Mr. Horn: 'All right, I'll have a cup of tea and come back at eight o'clock.'

W.J.: 'Very well, let's give this a try; but it really is a last hope. If you don't go tomorrow, Norman, I shan't come chasing you again. You've told me that you don't want that, so it's up to you. I'll tell the school to expect you tomorrow.'

Mrs Horn: 'That's if we haven't all taken a bottle of aspirins or something. I've had as much as I can take of it.'

W.J.: 'Well, goodbye then.'

(*Mr Horn follows me out, agreeing to play his part.*)

In fact, Norman went to school the following day and,

with the exception of one very difficult period, has been ever since. I shall return to this story later.

The important point about the interaction in this family is that although the bonds (of affection and of mutual need) which tie the members together stand out clearly, even in this situation, they are strenuously denied. Both Mrs Horn and Norman say they want to leave home; Mrs Horn says little else. Mr Horn does not threaten this, but he threatens to hit Norman (and frequently does). When they are under stress the family members look to escape from their links with each other as a means to a solution. Whereas the families of schizophrenics draw together and try to bury their differences, the centrifugal families fight and run.

Both the tendencies represented in the families of schizophrenics and those in the Horn family are present to some extent in every family group. Even the schizophrenic families have some centrifugal tendencies; in fact it was often the drive to establish some autonomous existence which would allow them to escape from the family's emotional bonds into the outside world that first led the daughters in Laing and Esterson's studies to be described by their parents as 'ill'. On the other side, there were many integrative forces at work in the Horn family; because of her own (denied) fears of the outside world Mrs Horn kept her children very close to her, and Norman in particular was very dependent on her. But just as the centrifugal pressures were the most difficult for the integrative families of schizophrenics to deal with, and it was these that led to the conflict and ultimately the 'illness', so in the centrifugal family the members' emotional needs for each other and the demands they made on each other were felt to be unbearable, dangerous and threatening things to be denied and escaped from as much as possible.

Thus both excessively integrative and excessively centrifugal families have some strengths as well as considerable weaknesses, but their greatest weaknesses are shown in

40

face of different situations. The weakness of the integrative family is in dealing with situations of difficulty which arise in its members' contacts with the world outside the family. Especially where the demands of such outside relationships conflict with members' roles within the family, the family group tends to tighten its grip on all its membership, to retreat into itself, and to try to compensate any member it has thus denied of social contact with the rest of the world by creating an ever more harmonious and complete set of social relations within the family. Certain members are thus forced to sacrifice all expression of those parts of their personalities which cannot effectively find expression within the family (for the daughters in Laing and Esterson's studies it was often their sexual needs that had to be denied) for the sake of integration and the mutual satisfaction of emotional needs in the family group.

The weaknesses of the centrifugal family are seen in quite other situations. First, where a member of the family needs to express feelings or to have emotional demands met within the family group, but the family cannot allow this, and insists that he should seek to satisfy these outside the group, then that member may carry these emotional needs over into outside relationships in a distorted way. Thus any emotional demand which the family, because of its fears about involvement at a feeling level between its members, cannot allow to be expressed or to be satisfied may be externalised by the rejected member. For instance, a child whose needs for affection are not met may steal symbols of this from others outside the family;[11] or a wife may carry over her unmet emotional demands on her husband into demanding and dependent relationships with outsiders; or a husband may express angry frustration with his wife in aggressive external relationships. These reactions have been noticed and well documented in the literature of social problems and of their treatment, even if they have not been related to the concept of centrifugal families as I have outlined it here.

Such phenomena are not always easy to recognise because of the cultural prohibition on the expression of emotional needs in centrifugal families. Members of such groups, when confronted with the apparent emotional content of their relationships with the outside world, and their seeming connection with needs that are not being met in the family, will usually deny these implications. It is about as difficult to get the emotional content in such behaviour accepted by a member of a centrifugal family as it is to get the social-centrifugal content in schizophrenic behaviour recognised in an integrative family.

Interaction in centrifugal families

However, particularly in the case of families with delinquent sons, there is another weakness which seems to exaggerate any tendency by a member (in this case the delinquent one) to compensate for unmet emotional needs in his external social behaviour. This is the reaction of the parents to emotional stress in their relationship, particularly if at the time one or both of them are to some extent being blocked from their normal channels of emotional release in activities outside the family. Such a situation quite frequently occurs in at least one parent's life during the teenage years of their children through menopausal problems, or death or serious illness of one of the grandparents, on whom the parent may well have heavily depended, or some other upheaval of the whole family group which disrupts social contacts. Suppose, for instance, the mother's mother dies at this time (or that the family is rehoused in another district, where patterns of contact between mother and grandmother cannot be maintained). In this kind of situation, the mother might, in other kinds of families, become more dependent on her husband, but in the culture of the centrifugal family such dependence may seem dangerous and threatening. Either the husband may seem too uninterested and remote in his own social world or the wife may be afraid of undermining his precarious masculinity by making emotional demands on him. The avoidance of emotional involvement in such families is usually based on a fear that the expression of or demand for strong feeling in the family group would tend to undermine stability and cause the breakdown of behaviour patterns which are appropriate to the roles of each member of the family.

I am suggesting here that there is within all families a kind of emotional *status quo*, a tacitly agreed partitioning of roles, each with its stereotype of behaviour and feeling content. In centrifugal families the stereotypes are particularly rigid and the feelings which are allowed to be expressed in each role very prescribed and limited. If the mother's is supposed to be a strong and independent role, a source of support to the rest of the family, an experience like the death of the grandmother or the loss of all her friends will threaten the whole emotional stability of the family. It creates needs in her which can neither be met inside the family nor outside it. In this situation, these needs may be denied and transmitted to other members of the family who can more safely express them (though often in a distorted way) in relationships outside the family. Thus, for instance, a very desperate form of escapist social activities by a teenage boy may reflect the emotional and social needs of his mother, which she is denying and transmitting to him, because he is in a far better position to satisfy these needs in his pattern of life than she is, and because disruptive as his behaviour may be (especially outside the family) it is not seen as a threat to the stability, or the very existence, of the family group in the way an expression of such feelings by his mother would be.

The transmission of feelings by a 'trapped' member of the family to another member who can externalise these feelings because of better access to the outside world is a product of a tacitly agreed concept of family life which sees all emotional conflict as more safely resolved in external relationships than within the group. Thus, the children frequently act out the emotional needs of the parents which conflict with their parental roles, and in centrifugal families this is felt to be a much safer kind of expression of feelings than would be possible if potentially conflicting emotional needs were expressed within the group.

Two examples of the contrasting reactions of integrative and centrifugal families in the face of a problem which contains a mixture of emotional and social difficulties, such as moving to a new area, could be represented diagrammatically. As is seen in the diagrammatic form of these examples, both patterns represent a disruptive invasion of the teenager's feelings and behaviour by the parents and in these instances particularly by the mother. Both follow from a situation which gives rise to a mixture of feelings in the mother, thus making conflicting demands upon her, which she cannot manage to resolve except through her child. In the first case, some of these feelings are projected on to the child in a confusing way; to the child are attributed fears of the outside world which she does not have (though her mother does) and the feelings she does have (of wanting to get out of the family, at least to some extent) she is told do not exist. In the second case, an existing pattern of the son's behaviour is intensified and exaggerated till it reaches a manic scale by the transmission from the mother of feelings that she fears are potentially destructive, and therefore denies. Both, too, are the result of emotional conflicts which might less harmfully in other families have been expressed openly in disagreements between the parents. However, in the integrative family, in which 'harmony' is seen as all important, and parents strive to keep up a front of agreeing on everything, and being totally satisfied with their life together, to the point of excluding the outside world, such open conflict would be seen as dangerous and destructive, and is therefore expressed in conflicting demands on the daughter. In the centrifugal family, the expression of the

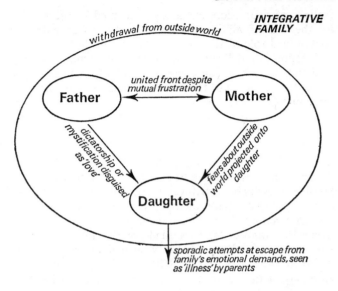

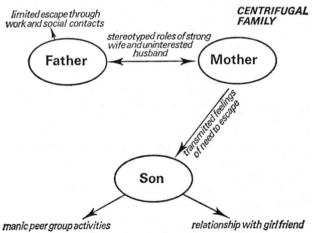

Figure 1 Reactions of an integrative and a centrifugal family to a problem

feelings of depression and anxiety aroused in the mother by the loss of all her friends, would conflict with her stereotyped role of the strong wife and mother and might undermine her delicately balanced relationship with her husband, so rather than cause a potentially dangerous upset in the *status quo*, the mother denies her feelings and transmits them to her son.

The Greenslade family

At this point I would like to give some examples of actual families in which centrifugal tendencies in face of fears about emotional involvement seem to have contributed to the delinquency of one of the teenage sons. The first is the Greenslade family. Mr Greenslade, who came up from a working-class background, but who had worked his way up to a position of responsibility in the firm which had employed him for many years, had met his wife at a dance. She came from another part of the country and was a quieter person than her husband, who had lived a gay social life before their meeting.

Twenty years later they had two teenage sons who were physically alike, but different in every other way. Robin, the elder, had done well at school and was about to embark on a career of which his father strongly approved. David (aged eighteen), on the other hand, had been difficult ever since failing his eleven plus. He had been anti-authority and unsuccessful at school, he had had two jobs before settling down in his third one, which was a manual trade, and he had a quarrelsome relationship with his father. David resented his father's 'interference' in his life, even though on investigation this appeared to take the form of an occasional disapproving remark about the amount of time he spent away from home and his choice of friends. In fact, David was nearly always away with gangs of his mates, who were usually the most delinquent in the area. He had twice been in trouble with the law

46

together with groups of these boys, and his father's efforts to keep him out of trouble seemed half-hearted and ineffectual, contrasting with David's strongly expressed resentment of what he seemed to feel as a real and unwanted attempt at exerting a controlling influence.

This description of the family pattern reflects what was happening at the time when David got into trouble for the third time, and was eventually sent for a short period of residential training. When I saw his parents before the court case, their attitudes towards David's offence contrasted vividly. Mr Greenslade, whom I saw first on his own, was initially absolutely furious about it, and threatening to throw David out of the house. He was both angry and hurt about David's actions, but as he talked about them, he became almost pathetic. He bemoaned the fact that David told him nothing about his activities away from home, and also that David was so openly hostile to him. Gradually he told me that David's was not the only hostility to him in the family. He said that his wife did not communicate with him either, that she was moody, sullen and silent, and told him little of her feelings. He said that she had announced David's fresh offence to him when he came home one Saturday evening after attending a works function. She had told him of it as if she was enjoying using it as a weapon to hit him over the head. Mr Greenslade said his wife refused to become involved in any of his social activities, which were numerous, that she seemed to resent everything about him and about her life with him, and that he felt hopeless and helpless to deal with her. Mr Greenslade, who was still a tall, fine-looking man, and who had at first seemed rather impressive, almost visibly shrank as he admitted all this to me. Soon after this, Mrs Greenslade came in, and talked to me alone. The emotional tone of her conversation was very different from her husband's. Although she said she was shocked about David's offence, her manner contrasted with her words. If anything, she seemed

47

to be triumphing in her husband's plight, and pleased to see him deflated.

When I saw them again together after David had been sent away, Mr Greenslade once more started with an impressive display of self-righteousness, and anger with the court for their action. He repeated that he could not understand the reason for David's hostility to him. At this, Mrs Greenslade, who had been sitting very quietly through quite a long speech by her husband, burst into the conversation saying, 'But of course, you never did like David as much as Robin.' Mr Greenslade protested feebly but looked completely deflated again. Mrs Greenslade followed this up with detailed evidence of his failures as a father. She quoted to me the neighbours' opinions, which were unanimous on the point that he had been hard on David and made a fuss of Robin. She went on to say that he had never taken any interest in either of the boys when they were younger, and that they had hardly known him until they were in their teens. He had been so busy with his social activities, with running the social club, the football club and various other activities outside the home that he had had no time for the children. Mr Greenslade had absolutely no answer to these damaging statements and could do no more than remark that they were 'only speculation'. When I asked Mrs Greenslade whether she too felt neglected by her husband, she confirmed this, saying that as soon as she had had the children she could not go out with him, and since then she had been virtually confined to the home by her responsibilities for them. In the next interview she took this further, saying that she very much resented living in Mr Greenslade's home town, which she regarded as much too quiet and dull, and lacking in all the amenities of a civilised existence. She had repeatedly tried to persuade him to move back to her home area, but he had always refused. She was thoroughly bored with her existence as a housewife, and resented the fact that her husband had made no sacrifices in his social life for the sake of the children, whereas she had given up everything that had given her pleasure in life.

When in both of these interviews I suggested to Mrs Greenslade that she tended to identify with David in his stand against her husband, she smilingly acknowledged this without guilt or hesitation, but with something of a knowing look, as if she was glad that at last someone appreciated the subtleties of her family's relationships. She did not even deny my suggestion that she half encouraged the bad aspects of David's behaviour, because of her own resentment towards her husband, and that when he did something wrong which hurt his father she could not really condemn him. In the second interview she mentioned that she was looking forward to David getting his motor cycle licence back (which he had lost through disqualification) so he could take her out on it occasionally. She acknowledged that the sort of things David did were just the sort of things she would like to do, if only she had the chance.

In subsequent interviews while David was away I tried to help Mr and Mrs Greenslade to talk about how they felt towards each other, but they found it very difficult to do so. Mrs Greenslade said that her husband just liked his way of life and was selfishly holding on to it, and Mr Greenslade insisted that his wife did not really want to change, but preferred to grumble about her lot. What stood out about their relationship was their sense of the impossibility of making real emotional contact with each other, based on a fear of doing so. Mr Greenslade seemed to see his wife as an alarmingly emotional person whose depression might drag him down with her; she seemed to sense his defensive insecurity, and to have given up any hope of getting through his shell. They had both allowed an unsatisfactory pattern to develop because they felt that there was no real alternative; a shared emotional life within the family was not a realistic expectation. David's exaggerated escapism was a reflection of their unresolved conflict.

In this family the centrifugal tendencies had left an emotional vacuum, reflected in the breakdown of communication between the parents, but it had not prevented the family from living an outwardly conventional and even apparently successful life, the only obvious flaw in which was David's delinquent behaviour. In the Price family, however, the same tendencies were part of a totally disruptive pattern.

The Price family

Mr Price came from a traditional, respectable working-class family in which high priority was given to honesty and hard work, but he had married a young woman with a very different background, who deceived him many times with other men before finally leaving him. He was left with five children, and by the time I got to know the family some six years after Mrs Price's desertion they were all in their teens. Mr Price, who in his relationship with his wife had alternated between trying to ignore her behaviour and losing his temper with her about it, still worked hard, as he had always done, to provide for his family. However, he never pretended that he could make up for his wife's absence, and seemed convinced of the impossibility of an adequate family life in these circumstances. Mr Price appeared never to have got over his wife leaving. For several years afterwards he tried to get her back devising plans for the whole family, including her, to live elsewhere. After this, he said he wanted to forget his wife, and to return to 'normal'. However, his definition of normality was in terms of respectability, and of his neighbours' opinions of the family's social behaviour. He blamed his wife and the children for the loss of the family's good name, and looked to the children to re-establish it by behaving better in the outside world. As far as family life was concerned, he sometimes talked of remarrying in order 'to give the kids some home life again', but never persisted in his relationships with other women, apparently because of the strong feelings he still had about his wife.

In this climate of opinion, it was not surprising that the children, who had had many unfortunate experiences while their mother was there, should drift away from home as much as possible, especially when their father was out at work. Mr Price alternated between ignoring their activities and rowing about them; in fact he re-created his relationship with his wife with them. They in turn tended to identify with their mother, and fought against him with her weapons. In quarrels between them, Mr Price would always start by threatening to give up the family home and have them 'put away', and they would instantly retaliate by saying they intended to move out into flats anyway. They were unable to depend on him, and he to accept their dependence, yet the whole group clung together as if sucked inward by the vacuum left when Mrs Price deserted them, struggling to escape from each other, unable to meet each other's needs, angry, quarrelsome, recriminating and yet unable to break free. It was as if Mrs Price, through their need for her and their anger about her leaving, still held them unwillingly together.

The children had been in various kinds of trouble, and two had been away from home for periods of residential training. Here is a conversation with one of them, Terry (aged eighteen), which expresses some of the centrifugal tendencies of the family.

Terry: 'Dad's always losing his temper.'

W.J.: 'What about?'

Terry: 'He just loses his bloody temper, about any little thing. If he comes in and the kids haven't washed up the dishes, he keeps on about it.'

W.J.: 'Why should he lose his temper?'

Terry: 'About those little things.'

W.J.: 'But when someone keeps losing his temper about little things, perhaps there's something bigger wrong.'

Terry: 'No, he just keeps losing his bloody temper, that's all.'

W.J.: 'You mean he's always been like that? Ever since your mother left?'

Terry: 'Oh, that was years ago. He's just bad tempered, that's all.'

W.J.: 'He's got a lot to cope with. What would you do if you were him?'

Terry: 'He shouldn't keep on so. Keep his bloody temper.'

W.J.: 'But what would you *do* different?'

Terry: 'I dunno. He just hangs around being miserable.'

W.J.: 'Why should he be miserable?'

Terry: 'Dunno. He never goes anywhere.'

W.J.: 'Would it help if he went out?'

Terry: 'I should think so!'

W.J.: 'Help who, him or you?'

Terry: 'Help him, I should think. Get away from this bloody place.'

W.J.: 'Why should he do that?'

Terry: 'Well, who wants to stay in this bloody place?'

W.J.: 'You go out as much as you can?'

Terry: 'I should think so. Can't stick around in this bloody place; drives you mad.'

W.J.: 'You get on each other's nerves if you stay in?'

Terry: 'Of course you bloody do. I go out when I can. Last Saturday I stayed home, did a few things in the morning. Then I lay down and fell asleep till 2 o'clock! I mean, that's what it's like, drives you mad, bloody kids everywhere.'

The Price family, partly because of the absent mother, represents a centrifugal family *par excellence*. Mr Price envies his wife her freedom, bemoans his enslavement and responsibilities to the children, dreams of a new social life, based on 'respect' in the outside world, and blames his wife and the children for his failure to find it. The children wander abroad, getting into trouble behind their father's back, threatening to leave home if he tries to control them in any way.

Finally, here is a less extreme example. A middle-aged couple had two children, the younger of whom was a boy aged fifteen. The wife had had a close relationship with her parents, both of whom had recently died. She herself had even more recently been seriously ill. The husband's parents had moved to another part of the country, so contact was infrequent. He had recently been subjected to increasing demands at work, which kept him involved there for more of his time than previously. He was prepared to suffer this for the sake of the family income, but it denied him any social life. Since the death of his wife's parents and the new demands on the husband, the boy had been a problem for them. He was apparently old beyond his years, and spent all his time away from home, in the company of a gang of older teenagers. When he got into trouble with the police, his parents said they were shocked, but their reaction was passive. They made no effort to control the boy, but simply said they could not understand him. They appeared to have given up any parental role, and he seemed to have stopped trying to communicate with them. The wife was ill and concentrated on domestic tasks; the husband overworked; the boy went on associating with the gang, boasting of their exploits, some of which were illegal. While he seemed to be asking for control, his parents appeared to be too ill and preoccupied to provide it.

Here the boy's apparently excessive fascination with gang activities which were beyond his age and maturity (he was the only one in the gang to get into trouble with the police) seemed to be related to his parents' frustration with their social isolation, imposed by external events. It seemed to be no coincidence that their son's exaggerated involvement in social activities outside the family started just when the parents were boxed in, and forced to stay within the confines of the nuclear family group. He was acting out what they felt was impossible for them. They could not control him because control would mean keeping him in the family; but for them family life meant frustration and illness. This would be too much of a punishment to impose on the boy. The boy was driven out with more freedom than he could cope with by forces within the family which seemed to say, 'Here is nothing but sickness and advancing age; get out while you're young.'

In centrifugal families like these, the drive to escape from the emotional nucleus of family life and to externalise their feelings may well take them to a social worker. The role of the social worker in such family situations is discussed in the next chapter.

References

1 G. P. Murdock, *Social Structure*, Macmillan, 1949.
2 P. Willmott and M. Young, *Family and Kinship in East London*, Routledge & Kegan Paul, 1957.
3 C. Rosser and C. Harris, *The Family and Social Change*, Routledge & Kegan Paul, 1965.
4 E. Bott, *Family and Social Network*, Tavistock, 1957.
5 C. Harris, *The Family*, Allen & Unwin, 1969.
6 T. Parsons, *The Social System*, Free Press, 1964.
7 W. J. Goode, *World Revolution and Family Patterns*, Free Press, 1963.
8 R. D. Laing and A. Esterson, *Sanity, Madness and the Family*: vol. 1, *Families of Schizophrenics*, Tavistock, 1964.
9 Harris, op. cit.
10 I. Bennett, *Delinquent and Neurotic Children. A Comparative Study*, Tavistock, 1960.
11 K. Friedlander, *The Psychoanalytical Approach to Juvenile Delinquency*, Routledge & Kegan Paul, 1947.

3

The role of the social worker

In the previous chapter I suggested that it was important to try to analyse the emotional content of family relationships in terms of the kinds of relationships which family members had with people outside the family, especially their relationships with their kin and with their wider social networks. In this chapter I shall suggest that just as the emotional content of relationships within the family group will be to a great extent determined by the quality of these external relationships, so the kind of relationship that the family makes with a social worker will also largely depend on these factors.

At this point it is worth looking at what is meant by 'the family' making a relationship. In the last chapter I frequently made such statements as 'the family feels ...' or 'the family fears ...', and it is necessary to say more about the sense in which a family can be said to do such things. In this context, 'the family feels' is a shorthand way of saying 'the shared attitude of the members of the family is' or 'the family consensus is'. As I pointed out in the first chapter, shared family norms are not often explicit or specific, and are likely to be established over a period of time, and constantly to be altered and reformed as relationships change and members grow older. However, there seems good reason to believe that families do come to have shared expectations of each other in certain situations, and also shared expectations of people outside the family. It is this latter point that is particularly important here, as the way that the family reacts to a social worker is likely to reflect their shared views about the kind of relationship which they can expect to make with someone from outside the family who is also an official.

That families do have such shared views among their membership, and that there are strongly similar views held by people of similar social backgrounds is well illustrated by the study made by Mayer and Timms of sixty working-class clients of the Family Welfare Association.[1] They found that most of the people they interviewed had an expectation of help based on a 'unicausal-moralistic-suppressive' approach to their problems in family relationships. For instance, in marital conflicts, both parties expected to present their case, and then to be told what was wrong, who was wrong, and what was to be done about the person who was in the wrong. But an important element in this expectation was the fact that most of the clients (nine out of ten) had at least one person to whom they usually turned when they had personal or family problems. Thus, the kind of relationship they made with the worker was very often based largely on the kind of help they were accustomed to receive from these informal sources.

This suggests that those families whose pattern of life involves the parents in frequent contacts with a close-knit network of supportive neighbours and relatives tend to find expression for much of their emotional life and deal with their problems outside the family through this network in rather the same, if not as extreme a way as the centrifugal families which I described in the last chapter. Unlike isolated integrative families, they tend to resolve emotional difficulties by activities outside the nuclear family group rather than in discussions among the family membership, and this is bound to affect their expectations of the role of the social worker.

It would therefore be misleading to try to analyse the emotional content of the relationship that a family makes with a social worker without considering its attitudes to other social, helpful or official relationships outside the family. If there is validity in the distinction I have made in the previous chapter between integrative and centrifugal patterns of family interaction, then these seem to represent opposite extremes in a scale which extends from those integrative families which set great store by emotional relationships, but are deeply suspicious of outsiders, to those centrifugal families which tend to shun emotional relationships but have high expectations of people outside the family group.

It is clear that these very different attitudes towards relationships outside the family must greatly influence what happens between the social worker and the family. The integrative family is unlikely to approach a social worker or any other outsider about the behaviour of any of its members until after every possible effort has been made, by means of discussion and emotional pressure, to restore the harmony which that behaviour threatens within the family group. The centrifugal family's members, however, may well have discussed their difficulties individually with other outsiders, but are unlikely to have faced up together to any of the emotional issues involved. Each type of family will seek to engage the worker in a continued search for the solution of its difficulties along the same lines as it has taken up to the time when he became involved.

Unless, therefore, we have a very high expectation of the worker's ability to control the situation and convert the family to his way of looking at it, the family's previous understanding of its difficulties and the methods it has adopted to try to overcome them are very important. In fact, I shall suggest that each type of family has a very strong effect on social workers, and exerts pressures on them to react in ways which do not undermine the patterns which the family, for its own purposes, has created. If social workers fail to take into account these ways in which such families seek to control them and the kind of help they give, they are likely either to be rejected or else to find themselves colluding with family patterns in a destructive way.

In this chapter I shall again concentrate mainly on centrifugal families, partly because I think that in most social work settings (other than mental health) there are more clients' families with centrifugal tendencies than there are with integrative tendencies, and partly because more has been written, mainly from the mental health point of view, about interaction in an integrative family, and the difficulties that such situations present.

Example of work with an integrative family: the Bascombes

In integrative families a social worker is nearly always brought into the situation because one member (usually one of the children) is trying to break out of the tightly-held family circle. The social worker's role then becomes in the family's eyes that of restoring harmony by persuading the 'sick' or 'bad' member that he would be much better if he only returned to the security and affection which his family are offering. Strong pressures are brought to bear on the social worker to become part of the family group itself, and to accept all the presuppositions of family life. He is made at home, treated like one of the family, given a special chair. Everything he says is agreed with, and taken as confirmation of what is already believed in the family. If he criticises what is going on, this too is accepted, and if he points out that another line of action or thought might be preferable, this is agreed with as well, and he is told that the family tried just this in 1939, but unfortunately it proved impossible. Gradually the social worker feels under more and more pressure to agree with the family's beliefs about life, to accept them all, or to get out. He is threatened in a subtle way that any change would be totally disruptive; things must stay just as they have always been. He must either give up the struggle to cause change or escape while he can.

I experienced something of this as a result of my contact

with Mr Bascombe. He was a man in his forties who had twice been before courts for offences of indecent assault on boys. When he first came to see me his main reason seemed to be his resentment of police interference in his life. He complained that he was harassed by the police quite unnecessarily, and seemed to want to lead a quiet life, with freedom to have 'innocent' associations with boys. However, as he talked about his life it seemed that he had other reasons to feel dissatisfied and resentful as well. One of these was that he had made several attempts to get help to change his way of life, particularly to overcome his feelings of attraction to teenage boys. He was as angry with people who had either promised to help and done nothing, or told him not to worry about his feelings, as he was with those who condemned him and treated him as an outcast. He seemed to have thoroughly mixed feelings about his friendships with boys, being uncertain whether to defend these as innocent and natural, or attempt to escape from the danger and insecurity they caused him, as well as his own condemnation of their strong sexual content.

As he discussed how he came to be involved with boys, it seemed that he had never had the opportunity to develop mature relationships because of his ties to his mother. The two of them lived together, and his mother completely controlled his life, mainly by stressing to him how much they needed each other. Emotionally he was still a boy, and his relationships with boys were his only escape from his mother. Only very slowly did he express resentment about his ties to his mother, and the way in which she imposed these on him. After we had discussed these matters over the course of many interviews, I suggested that I might meet his mother, but it was a long time before he eventually agreed. Again, on this subject, his mixed feelings were vividly expressed as he alternated between apparent hope that I would somehow magically break his ties with his mother, and fear that I would intrude roughly into his home and shatter his security, breaking

59

down the pattern of his relationship with his mother which had been unchanged for over twenty years.

I felt very anxious when I finally met Mrs Bascombe, but she was both welcoming and charming. She greeted me with a smile and invited me in hospitably. At first she was inquisitive about my involvement with her son, but once she had established that I was not a policeman she talked quite freely about him, stressing how badly he had been treated. She then quite firmly stated her view of his best answer to his situation—keeping to himself —challenging me to dare to disagree with an aggressive, 'What do you think?' When I wondered if he sometimes felt he had missed some things in life, she said with some emphasis that he was quite happy at home nearly all the time, except when in one of his 'moods', which she attributed to 'his difficult age'. Whenever any difficulty was mentioned she would discuss this for a moment, and then dismiss it with a smiling but aggressive, 'But then, what can I do about it?' In my second interview with her she was even more expansive, talking about her early life, her marriage, her husband's death and her son's childhood. She treated the development of their life together up to the present day as a natural progression, complicated only by the intervention of certain outside factors. They had both been persecuted and badly treated. She made it clear that she thought that her son, like herself, must accept the life they had together as both inevitable and unalterable. After all, 'What else is there?' Any restlessness on his part was 'just his age'.

When I saw Mrs Bascombe and her son for the first time together (after knowing him for well over a year) it was immediately clear that there was no hope of his expressing any dissent from his mother's point of view. Nearly the whole of the first two interviews I had with them was taken up by them both telling me (taking turns) the story of how badly they had been treated by one of their landlords. He had made their life unbearable by repeated invasions of their privacy which had undermined their security and happiness. I felt totally identified with this evil being, and the force of their unanimity in rejecting such a monster had a powerful effect on me. They made it quite clear that the only result of this persecution had been to drive them more closely together, and increase their need for each other, and that the threat of such happenings in the future made it imperative that they should stay close and be watchful. They described their life as if their home was in a state of siege. Mr Bascombe agreed with every word his mother said, and she finished her account of every episode with, 'Isn't that right, Roger?'

It was only in my third conversation with them together that I was able even to touch on the grounds for potential disagreement between them, but Mrs Bascombe dealt summarily with any hint of discord or a clash of interests between herself and her son. Although he looked a little uncomfortable at times, he clearly dared not contest the issue, and seemed genuinely to feel identified with his mother against the possibilities of change in face of which his enormous fears overwhelmed the shadowy hopes which he had confided to me in my office.

Mrs Bascombe contrasted the wicked landlord with the kindly county court judge who had helped them achieve a fresh security in their new home, and she made it plain to me that my choice was between these roles. If I came between them or tried to change their life, they would fight me, and they would win. I was given an alternative, to be their ally against their persecutors in the outside world. There was, she seemed to say, no third role.

I still don't know what else I could have done. One idea would have been to import another social worker, who could have given voice more definitely to Mr Bascombe's unspoken objections to his mother's all-powerful view of the situation. Perhaps gradually a kind of identification between Mr Bascombe and his spokesman could have been achieved, while I held the balance and tried to recognise Mrs Bascombe's needs and help her cope with her feelings. But to do this I would have had to be more sure that Mr Bascombe could carry through his bid for independence and maturity than I was.

These difficulties are the ones that I feel are characteristic of a social worker's dealings with an integrative family. The worker may start by seeing himself as a force for constructive change, but he is soon confronted with the family's view of change as dangerous and destructive. He may feel he wants to support the glimmer of dissent that can be recognised in one member's behaviour, but he will discover that that member may quickly seek refuge within the family consensus once the pressure is put on him, thus putting the worker in the role of unnecessary troublemaker or seditious conspirator. Thus the worker is seemingly forced to choose between being an unacceptable outsider or an affable insider; between collusion or damaging conflict. I do not propose to write about possible solutions to this dilemma, as there are many others who can do this better than myself. Instead, I shall describe the very contrasting pressures brought to bear by centrifugal families on social workers who become involved with them.

Problems of working with centrifugal families

I have described in the previous chapter how centrifugal families seek to externalise the feelings which lie at the core of family life, because they fear the force of these feelings, and suspect they cannot bear them. In order to protect themselves against these feelings, they define family roles, and the emotions which are appropriately expressed in them, in relatively rigid and stereotyped ways. On the other hand, they give plenty of scope and encouragement to the free expression of feelings and the satisfaction of emotional needs in social activities away from the family group, and each member tries to acquire a social network in which these can take place. However, where a particular member is subjected to a great deal of emotional stress, or is denied an outlet to the outside world, the pattern of family interaction may permit feelings which are felt to

62

be threatening to the family's security to be expressed by another member of the family, who has access to a social network, in outside relationships. Thus, particularly if one of the parents has feelings which are feared might disrupt the whole functioning of the family if they were expressed within it, these feelings may be transmitted to a teenage child who has a better opportunity of acting them out. I have given examples of delinquent boys doing things on behalf of their parents. It would have been equally possible to give examples of promiscuous teenage girls expressing their mothers' sexual feelings which were being denied for the sake of family stability; or of illegitimate babies born to teenage daughters after their mothers had been obliged to stop having more children.

However, such patterns of interaction do cause social problems. In the first place, the whole culture of centrifugal families tends to drive their teenage children out into the big world outside the family before they are emotionally ready for it. Because such families play down dependency and mutual need in the family group, they encourage children to overestimate their independence and ability to fend for themselves away from home. Furthermore, such a pattern becomes much more likely to bring about unacceptable behaviour by the adolescent members of these families if it is reinforced by the transmission of feelings from parents to their children. A teenager who is acting out a 'double dose' of feelings on behalf of his parents as well as himself (in the way David Greenslade was) is very likely to behave in ways which are difficult for other people to tolerate. The mixture of a denial of all feelings connected with dependence and family ties, together with an exaggerated search for social satisfactions, is characteristic of the personalities of teenage members of centrifugal families.

Where this occurs, social workers are very likely to become involved with the family because of other people's disapproval of the teenage member's behaviour. This puts the family in a very difficult position. They themselves may be concerned about their adolescent's extremism, and they may in some way have some guilty suspicions that its origin is not unconnected with themselves. However, it is very important to them to maintain the emotional *status quo* in the family, and to make sure that the feelings represented by the child's behaviour continue to be expressed outside the family and not within it. They are likely therefore to see the social worker both as a potential threat, in that he might try to stir up dangerous feelings in the family group, and also as potential means to a more secure situation. If the family can use the social worker as a way of externalising these feelings more completely, then they will be even safer than before; if he brings them nearer to them then they are in greater danger. It is the external, secure role that they seek to impose on him. They engage in a defensive manoeuvre, to support the *status quo* and ensure themselves against the invasion of feelings that they fear.

For such a family, the social worker's intervention is often sensed as helpful in a number of ways. First of all, he can apparently control the adolescent member of the family more effectively. The parents' own difficulty is that they cannot tell their child to stay in more with any conviction, partly because they do not wish to encourage his dependence, partly because they see family life as a damaging restriction on him, partly because they need him to be their representative in the outside world. The most they can do is tell him to behave better when he is out there; the social worker, with his greater authority, is apparently able to do this more effectively. Secondly, the social worker is seen as someone who is going to take a personal interest in the adolescent member of the family. Many parents in centrifugal families express the belief that 'he'll talk better to you, tell you things he can't tell me'. What they mean by this is presumably that the social worker will be more prepared to make emotional contact with their child than they are, more ready to accept his dependence and affection, and more ready to provide consistency, attention and concern in exchange. Such parents both doubt their ability to do this for their children, and fear the consequences of doing it within the family group. For an outsider to provide such a relationship with one of their children appears to be the solution to their difficulties.

Thus is created the characteristic pattern of supervision by social workers of the children of centrifugal families. The pattern is based on an attempt (not always very successful) at a relationship with the adolescent member based on both control and concern, a mixture of discipline and emotional guidance, combined with 'co-operation' with the parents consisting of an occasional discussion of general issues. In effect, it is a splitting off of the difficult member from the family group, in response to the family's defensive manoeuvre, first to ensure that all the feelings represented by the child's behaviour are kept outside the family group, and secondly to get rid of the parts of their parental roles they find most difficult, and give them to somebody else. This pattern is quite simply a response by the social worker to pressure by the family to behave in the way which most protects it against the forces it fears.

The trouble about such splitting off of the difficult member, and the assumption of a quasi-parental role by the social worker, is that it sets a dangerous precedent. Of course in a great number of cases this kind of work is 'successful', in that the adolescent gets in no further trouble (one sometimes wonders in such cases whether he would have anyway). On the other hand, if further crises do arise, the social worker has apparently committed himself in one direction. By accepting a partial parental role and the splitting off of the difficult member of the family, he seems to be saying that further trouble will lead to a further move in this direction. Thus he is partially committing himself to colluding with the pressures in such families to split off difficult members altogether, by means of 'sending them away'. In centrifugal families the method of separation is seen as the final safety route, the last avenue of escape from emotionally-charged situations in the family

65

group. It is the use of separations, and of institutions such as hospitals, children's homes and approved schools as the means of achieving them, that represents one of the most difficult pressures which such families bring to bear on social workers.

Pressure for separation

In some centrifugal families, separations have become part of the pattern of life, and are seen as a necessary and desirable way of ensuring a degree of security. The underlying assumption seems to be, 'if we didn't get a break from each other now and then, something really bad would happen which might split us up altogether. At least this way we get a chance to start again later on!' Some families are able to do this quite constructively by the use of kinship networks or close friends, with whom refuge can be taken when the pressure is on. But in other families which do not have such good opportunities for escape from each other, there can come to be an identification of safety and protection from dangerous feelings with various kinds of institutions, access to which is controlled, to some extent at least, by social workers. There are families in which one parent is repeatedly in and out of hospital or prison, or the children are frequently in care, or one by one depart for approved school when they reach the age of fourteen.

Such families represent an alarming challenge to social workers. On the one hand, patterns like this are precisely what social workers are there to prevent, under the Mental Health Act, the Probation of Offenders Act or the Children and Young Persons Act. Such behaviour represents a rejection of everything that social work stands for. Yet on the other hand, such people see social workers as holding the very keys to their security, for without the protection they get from such institutions they fear that they and their families will disintegrate completely. They therefore approach social workers in times of emo-

66

tional crisis with very strong pressure for protection from the feelings they most fear, demanding refuge in some place away from the family until the storm passes. They invest the social worker with this power to save them, yet at the same time they intimidate him with the fears that are threatening to overwhelm them. In working with members of centrifugal families at such moments, when separations are seen as the only means of safety, the worker feels under a terrible pressure to give his assent to their request, and to give them the protection they ask. He feels convinced without rational or objective thought about the subject (this comes later, in justification) that he must do as they suggest. He is invaded with the clients' fears of the alternative as totally destructive and catastrophic.

I suppose that the issue of how people in such a desperate state of mind can best be helped will always be one of the most hotly contested in social work. It is right that it should be, because if social work is not geared to helping such people in this kind of situation, then it is clearly failing in the task it has set itself. However, the issues involved in any debate on this subject tend to get obscured by all kinds of complicated factors. Not the least of these is the wide variation between the available provision in those social work departments which give priority to 'keeping the family together' at all costs, and that of those which 'relieve family distress' by providing facilities for short-term separations.[2] The presence or absence of facilities among a department's resources may give pragmatic justifications for policies after the original ardour which accompanied their introduction has disappeared, and tends to give each side in this particular argument a vested interest in their point of view.

An equally important complicating factor which is usually left out of the discussion of this problem is the personality of the social worker himself. Members of centrifugal families who come in distress to social workers are quite likely to represent a totally alien kind of emotional force from that which the worker has been accustomed to in his private life. It would be an absurd generalisation to suggest that most social workers grew up in relatively integrative families, but in so far as few middle-class families are as extremely centrifugal as the ones I have quoted, such behaviour is likely to be at least unfamiliar to a newly appointed worker. The whole ethos of social work appears to be basically integrative, particularly in relation to family life. Difficulties should be discussed, ironed out, minimised. Family members should learn to compromise, to give way, to demand less and give more within the family. Everything can be solved by talking it out and reaching a consensus. These are the kinds of presuppositions with which most social workers start in their jobs, and it is a rude shock to find that many clients do not share them. With some, it is true, an appeal to their finer instincts is effective. But others seem to rule out the very possibility of discussion and agreement between family members right from the start. They reject every casework principle out of hand. It is only natural that a worker who finds such behaviour alarming and unfamiliar should lack the confidence to challenge it, and should prefer to play safe by doing what is asked of him.

Furthermore, he can find justification for such a safety-first policy from most of the textbooks on casework. 'Methods of casework' tend to be divided between those which promote insight and those which lend support. Stern warnings are issued about trying to promote insight amongst those who are unready for it. Anxious, impulsive, acting-out people are the most unready, and the most needing of support. What could be more supportive than protecting them from the things they fear? It is thus with the blessing of the theorists that social workers acquire the habit, born of fear but gradually attaining a studied indifference, of colluding with the centrifugal tendencies of the most alarming of their clients.

The terrible weakness of such an approach is its tendency to confirm people's worst fears about themselves, and to reinforce patterns which are in the long run destructive. Each reception into care, each hospitalisation, each imprisonment on its own might be seen as a merciful release; but the danger of the first one is that it sets a precedent by confirming for the family that this is the only way to solve their problems. The danger is that each time an emotional difficulty in the family reappears, the same solution, or some escalated version of it, will be sought. If people are told in what is done for them, if not in words, that they are too bad or too inadequate to live their lives without this kind of protection by the authorities through their institutions, the danger is that they will become totally dependent on them for the whole pattern of a thoroughly miserable existence. A wife who has to go to a mental hospital twice a year is hardly being helped to lead a good life, any more than a family whose children one by one are sent to approved school is being helped to provide better care for its offspring.

The trouble with this kind of criticism of the collusive approach to work with centrifugal families, is that it is immediately suspected of representing another equally destructive and unhelpful approach to social work in these situations. This approach is based on 'casework' and bureaucratic blocking. It consists in a sort of passive resistance to the kind of pressures such people exert, combined with a shutting out of all the feelings that this would cause in a normal human being. It assumes that people who try to run away from their problems have something psychologically wrong with them, that can only possibly be put right by frustrating their efforts to do so and asking them difficult questions about their family relationships. It presents to the client the face of bureaucratic unhelpfulness, though behind his back it is likely to indulge in elaborate diagnostic speculation about his 'inadequacy' or 'immaturity'. It may drive the family to a desperate action, worsening their situation, as a kind of last despairing attempt to get the worker to recognise their plight, to penetrate an apparent wall of official indifference. Families

69

which really do desert or ill-treat children in the face of
this approach are frequently used as justifications for the
other, collusive one. Giving in to what the client wants,
in spite of reservations about the long-term consequences,
is seen as better than professional obduracy, leading to
total mutual frustration.

Social and economic pressures on the centrifugal family

It is this approach based on 'casework' and bureaucratic
blocking that has quite justifiably come in for some harsh
criticism from radical social workers,[3] who represent a
third point of view in this argument. They point out that
this technique can be very effectively used to ward off
the claims of people with real material and environmental
problems, and that in doing this social workers are protecting established authorities from the justifiable protests
of the poor and badly housed. Furthermore, once social
workers start to analyse all social problems in terms of
psychological deficiencies, it is a short step from this to
seeing all poor and disadvantaged people as maladjusted,
and more casework as the only possible solution to their
problems. They satirise the caseworker's single-minded
Freudianism as a well disguised form of social control, and
suggest that social workers should not only be more aware
of the material and environmental factors in social problems, but should also seek to encourage people to look
beyond their immediate difficulties, and to recognise that
the solution to their social problems may be in group or
community action, directed at asserting their economic and
social rights to a better life against those whose interests
are in keeping them down.

This radical line of thought has one important characteristic in common with those other approaches to social
work. This is that it involves trying to get people to look
at their social problems in a way that they have hitherto
been unable or unwilling to do. Social work has always
contained this element of wanting to change the client's

understanding of his situation as a means of achieving his betterment, and radicals are thus no exception. Poor and disadvantaged people are usually disorganised, and have little faith in their power to change their situation. It will therefore require a great deal of skill for this approach to bear fruit, and people themselves will not always welcome it or recognise it as the obvious answer to their problems. If groups of socially deprived people can be helped to seek this kind of solution it will be a major achievement, and social work will be a much richer and more constructive force in the communities it serves if this method of work can be more widely employed.

However there is a real danger of a split in social work between 'community workers' who are engaged in these or other activities with groups of people who are not necessarily clients, and caseworkers who are engaged in doing all the same old things to their clients. If this split occurs it is likely that the kind of people who were clients of caseworkers under the old regime will still be clients of caseworkers under the new regime, and will continue to be bureaucratically blocked or colluded with, according to the particular style of the agency.

The reasons for this are basically the same reasons that the vast majority of people who are poor or badly housed or socially disadvantaged in other ways do not become clients under the existing framework of social work provision. It seems to be the case that most people whose social problems are mainly material and environmental are too proud and independent to seek help with them from social workers, and that they quite realistically perceive that social workers are not likely to be much help in solving that kind of problem anyway. Thus those who do come to social workers are only those who are absolutely helpless (for instance, as a result of homelessness) or else those who have some other strong reason for wanting contact with such a person. I have suggested that one such reason is a powerful drive in centrifugal families to externalise their family problems. Among people who habitually go to 'the Welfare' with their difficulties are many who feel that social workers represent the only possible way to escape from certain dangerous forces in family life. Thus the social worker becomes the unwilling external recipient of the family's emotional problems, however much he may try to avoid this role. The choice of a social worker to turn to, rather than some other official (and there usually is some choice) is often determined by the emotional nature of the problem. Although the family apparently reject casework as a form of help, because they do not want to have their emotional problem put back into the family again, they still see the social worker as the appropriate authority, because feelings can only be externalised through a relationship, and this (to some limited degree at least) is what social workers offer.

Thus the danger of a split between community workers and caseworkers cannot altogether be overcome simply by converting caseworkers to a radical approach to social problems. However ideologically attractive the idea that social problems are the result of iniquitous material conditions may be, there is much evidence that some family problems exist which do not arise solely from environmental stress. There is thus a danger that community workers and radicals will concentrate their efforts on the 'independent' poor, who are more likely to respond to the notion of combining together to help themselves, while caseworkers are left to deal with those who experience their greatest difficulties in the emotional problems of family life, and who are thus so preoccupied with these that they are not free to participate in group or community action. In order that there should not be two kinds of social work, with two separate clienteles, it is necessary to establish methods of family casework which are ethically consistent with those of community work, and which also make the best possible use of the positive forces within the community generated by the efforts of community workers.

Facing emotional conflict with centrifugal families

My suggestion is that, just as in community work it is important to help people to recognise that what seems to be their individual problem is in fact a shared problem, and that it can have no real solution except through joint action, so in family work it is vital to help the family to discover that emotional problems, however alarming to them, are frequently the kind of problems that can only be settled among themselves, in the family, and at an emotional level. To help such a family to recognise and face this requires less skill in manipulating words and spotting distorted communications than courage to throw people back on their own resources who are terrified that their own resources are very weak. Just as the socially disadvantaged, conscious of the weakness of their group's position, come as individuals to the authorities, hoping to have their battles fought for them, so those who most fear their feelings come to social workers who are seen as capable of handling them. Just as the former can often only really be helped as a group by being turned back on their own group resources, weak as they seem, so the latter can only be helped by being led in the direction of facing up to what they most fear. It is very hard to turn someone back on what they are trying to escape from; to help them recognise in themselves what they are trying to externalise. The helping part of such a process is sharing the fear and the pain of what happens when the confrontation takes place, just as in working with groups of socially deprived people true help lies in sharing some of the social risks involved in standing up for their rights. If the social worker stands to lose nothing in what is undertaken in a desperate situation, then he cannot really be investing much in helping. In the emotional crises of a centrifugal family he, like them, may be physically at risk. In the economic, social or political battles of deprived groups he may stand to lose his job. If he is not willing to do either of these things, is he really earning his pay?

73

It is only in such situations that it is possible to distinguish between a social worker who really wants to help people, and one who is content to act as an agent of bureaucratic delay or social control. For a centrifugal family, when it does face its emotional problems, is likely to do so with violence, with tears, or with wild actions. If the social worker hasn't the courage to be on the scene when such things are happening, then he has no right to expect the family to be brave in face of their difficulties. It is only by showing them that he is not afraid to share the consequences of their all-powerful feelings that he can help them to experience as emotional and internal to the family the things they would otherwise have tried to put outside themselves.

To evolve a common philosophy for community work and family work may be easier than framing a common plan of action, for although there is a danger that if social work became split between these two branches there would be no overlap in their methods, there is no doubt that many people with emotional difficulties also have very great material problems as well. It should therefore be the task of family workers to enable people to overcome their emotional difficulties sufficiently to participate in the activities of their community group, and also to look for ways in which such participation can help their clients deal with the very emotional problems that they fear. This is obviously particularly important for centrifugal families, for whom social and group activities have such strong emotional significance. Having said this, I must now go on to illustrate just how difficult it is to put such principles into practice. The example of the Gray family, a centrifugal family who depended on separations for their precarious survival, shows this only too well.

The Gray family

When I first got to know them, Mr Gray was twenty-eight and Mrs Gray twenty-two, and they had been married for over two years. Mr Gray came from a local family which had several problem members. At the age of eleven he had been sent to approved school for a trifling offence. His father had requested this action of the court, and Mr Gray's feelings of hurt and anger about this were heavily overladen with opposing feelings that it had 'done him good', 'given the family a break' and 'been the making of him'. Since that time he had developed into a big, strong, hardworking man, who had been in no further trouble until just before I met him, when he had committed two minor offences in quick succession, both in pubs, on two of his frequent nights out with his mates.

Mrs Gray was an orphan who had been brought up by her widowed aunt. When she was a teenager she had been removed from her aunt's care under a fit person order because of the persistent cruelty with which she was being treated. Her aunt used her as a drudge, and she was forced to do all the domestic chores after her day's school was over; in addition to this she was frequently severely beaten and locked in her room for long periods. She told me that the first time this came to the notice of the authorities her aunt had succeeded in disguising the true situation, but the second time, because of obvious injuries to Mrs Gray, she had been immediately removed from home. She remembered this as a rescue, but she had mixed feelings about her period in care. On the one hand, it was for part of the time the period of greatest freedom in her life, when she had been able to enjoy the company of other girls, and indulged in many wild escapades. On the other hand, this had frequently got her into trouble, and she had had many moves from place to place, several of which were designed to restrict her freedom, and which included some that virtually recreated the conditions of her home life with her aunt. Mrs Gray had been happy to escape from a residential job into marriage at the end of her time in care.

However, both Mr and Mrs Gray were by then openly dissatisfied with their marriage. They had one daughter,

Susan, aged eighteen months. Mr Gray criticised his wife as slovenly, dirty and a bad mother. His grounds for the last criticism were mainly the fact that Susan was often allowed to get dirty and to make the place untidy. Mr Gray admitted that he was occasionally violent to his wife, but he insisted that she provoked him to this by her laziness and bad habits. Mrs Gray felt neglected by her husband. She said he worked long hours, and spent most evenings in pubs with his mates. He often went away for the weekend as well. When he was home he was critical and unhelpful. Everything had to be in order, and he would have nothing to do with Susan unless she was spotlessly clean. He never took his wife out with him, and she felt very lonely and cut off from other people.

The couple lived in a tiny upstairs flat, in poor structural condition, and of inconvenient design. The kitchen was barely a room at all, and the sitting-room was some distance away from it, up some stairs. I noticed very early in my contact with the family that Susan seemed to spend the whole day isolated from her mother in the sitting-room. The door of the sitting-room was usually locked; Mrs Gray justified this by saying that she was afraid of Susan falling down the stairs.

At the age of twelve months Susan had been admitted to hospital for the first time, and she had had several admissions since then. Her behaviour was very timid, and she seemed totally withdrawn, in a world of her own. She sat back all day on a settee, often banging her head against the back of it. She was a tall child for her age, and very pretty, but she seemed to make no contact with people, and would not play with toys. The medical authorities were 'investigating' Susan's condition. Some of her admissions to hospital had been on these grounds; others had been at Mrs Gray's request, because of 'convulsions'.

Mr and Mrs Gray blamed the flat for their difficulties with each other, and with Susan. They said that life in the flat gave them no chance, and Mr Gray quoted the cramped conditions as his reason for going out so much.

He needed to escape. Mrs Gray used the same conditions to justify her untidiness. She said there was no hope of keeping a place like that clean. As for Susan, Mrs Gray had a guilty awareness that the way she isolated Susan contributed substantially to her 'illness'. But this, too, was because of the flat. Mrs Gray pointed out that it was impossible to have Susan with her in the kitchen when she was doing her work. The sitting-room was the only place where she could be safe, behind a locked door.

Both parents had terribly mixed feelings about Susan's repeated removals to hospital. On the one hand they sensed strongly that these represented some kind of condemnation of their care of Susan, and although the medical authorities had never openly criticised them, they felt they had failed as parents. On the other hand, they found Susan very difficult to handle, and insisted that from time to time it was necessary, for her sake as well as theirs, to 'have a break'. Mrs Gray was very frightened of hitting Susan and hurting her when she had 'one of her tantrums', and she felt hospitalisation was often the only means of protecting Susan from her violent anger. Mr Gray was very concerned about the effect on Susan of seeing them quarrel and fight, as they frequently did. He felt that going to hospital was better for Susan than suffering this. In fact, her 'convulsions' often coincided with rows between them, and they could recognise that in this way she was being the scapegoat for their difficulties.

There was obviously a great deal of justification in Mr and Mrs Gray's claims that their problems were closely related to the appallingly inadequate accommodation in which they were living. In particular, Mrs Gray was very much isolated from her friends and relatives, and found it very difficult to leave the flat. However, their difficulties were greatly increased in this situation because of the strong centrifugal forces in the family. Mr Gray found family life with a child dirty, revolting and frightening (he was physically sick at the sight of a dirty nappy). He sought the maximum escape from it by means of his

77

social life; he also escaped from his own depression, laziness and dirtiness by transmitting them to his wife. Mrs Gray was terrified by the demands made on her by Susan. She felt quite unable to meet Susan's needs for attention and affection; having never been given these herself. Her locking away of Susan was to protect her from these demands. At the same time she felt neglected by her husband, and resented his failure to help her with Susan. But she could only express this resentment in her neglect of the home and her failure to carry out his demands, thus recreating her relationship with her aunt. She transmitted all her anger to him, and played the role of an ill-used Cinderella, the only one for which her upbringing had equipped her.

I was deeply affected by Susan's plight in this situation. I tried hard to help Mr and Mrs Gray get the council house they needed, but this was not easy, because of the waiting list and because Mr Gray's family had not been particularly good tenants. At the same time, I tried to help them face their fears about each other, and about the demands that family life with Susan made on them both.

This was very difficult because of what they represented to each other; Mr Gray seeing his wife as the personification of depression and dirtiness, Mrs Gray identifying her husband with her earlier neglect and ill-treatment. The only things they agreed about were the bad effect of the flat on them all, and the necessity of an occasional 'break' as the only answer to family pressures. Mr Gray got his breaks by going away at weekends, but Mrs Gray could only get hers by having Susan admitted to hospital. She could partially recognise the sort of effect this had on Susan's relationship with her, but her fear of the alternative, of hurting, or even killing Susan, was greater than her guilt about separations.

Because of the immense difficulties of getting Mr and Mrs Gray to look at their feelings, and because of the terrible damage I felt this pattern was doing to Susan, I tried to help Mrs Gray in practical ways. I made some arrangements which could have enabled her to go out more often. However, these were unproductive because of her dread of being 'shown up' by Susan making a scene in a crowded place. She feared the public exposure of her inability to meet Susan's demands. I also drew attention to the fact that the locked sitting-room door was unnecessary. By putting a low barrier across the stairs, Mrs Gray could keep Susan safe, yet within sight and earshot. Months after I had made this suggestion to Mr and Mrs Gray, and many excuses later, I actually put up such a movable barrier myself, with their consent (I am the world's worst carpenter). In fact, in spite of the surprising efficiency of this contraption it was never used. Mrs Gray couldn't bear to see or hear her daughter. Instead, Susan was sent to hospital twice more during the first year I knew the family, and she made little progress. Her diagnosis was (at this stage) possibly autistic, possibly spastic, probably subnormal.

At the end of this year, Mrs Gray went away for a weekend to stay with a friend of hers (who was working at the time as a striptease dancer) and committed an offence of stealing. Although this got her into trouble, it was also the start of a welcome fight back by her against the miserable existence she had been living. Soon after returning, she told me that she had reproached her husband for being out so much, had stood up to him when he hit her, had followed him when he went out, and had again stood her ground when he hit her in front of some other people. I recognised that she was asking for some support in her determination not to accept the pattern into which her life had drifted. She didn't want to leave her husband, but she wanted a better life with him. She acknowledged that her use of neglecting the house and passive resistance had been futile, and that her only real chance of getting her husband to change lay in making the best life she could for herself, rather than provoking more punishment from him and dreaming of escape that was beyond her reach.

Soon after this the family got their council house at last. At first everything was wonderful, and Mrs Gray was like a Cinderella whose dreams had come true. However, within two months she was pregnant again, and the improvements which had started to take place in both her relationships with her husband and with Susan began to vanish. Susan had made a good start in the new house, seeming much happier and more ready to play with her toys, and Mrs Gray could let her share her new kitchen. But as soon as she got pregnant Mrs Gray withdrew from her, and she became tearful and unresponsive again. At first she talked of Susan having to go back to hospital again, but when I plucked up the courage to point out that Susan's deterioration seemed to reflect her own state of mind since finding out about her pregnancy, to my surprise and relief she seemed able to accept this and to look for alternative solutions.

In fact, soon after this Mrs Gray recovered her good spirits, and once the difficult first three months of her pregnancy were over she seemed to blossom again. It was as if the pregnancy had been a reaction to her new happiness and freedom, which she had been determined to throw away, but now she reached out for them again, and to a considerable extent she found them. She redecorated the house, paid more attention to her appearance, and was rewarded by gaining much more notice from her husband who even started taking her out some evenings. She had friends who called, and instead of complaining to them, she allowed herself to enjoy their company. Above all, there was a tremendous improvement in her relationship with Susan. She had started taking Susan to a playgroup, and this was a great success. Not only did this give Mrs Gray her break, but it also helped Susan, who formed a good relationship with the playgroup leader, and began to develop quickly. Her relationship with her mother flourished, and there seemed to be the beginnings of affection expressed by both of them for each other.

However, hanging over all this progress was the threat

of the new baby, and the effect it would have on Mrs Gray's life. When it was born, everything went wrong. The baby was suspected of having a rare disease for a while, which worried Mrs Gray and made her ill. Mr Gray reacted unsympathetically to her and was, as before, disgusted with the baby. Furious quarrels developed between them, in which they both threatened to leave each other, and both got as far as walking out. In the midst of all this, Susan was removed from home by the medical authorities at Mrs Gray's request. Once again, when Mrs Gray was depressed and unable to bear the strain of family life, when her husband reacted by anger and by partial desertion, it was Susan who was finally forced to leave. It was only in this way their precarious marriage and what security it offered to them could be preserved.

As soon as Susan was in hospital, Mrs Gray's depression started to lift. She felt guilty about what had happened to Susan, but rather than dwell on this I decided to try to help her to establish a more satisfactory life again, believing that this was her best chance of re-establishing her relationships with her husband and Susan. I took her on shopping trips and tried to combine these with visits to Susan in hospital. She cheered up a great deal and soon had Susan back home again. Because of the new baby Mrs Gray could no longer take Susan to the playgroup, and the health authorities were dragging their feet about providing transport, so I took Susan myself, which after a few weeks seemed to shame them into arranging it. Susan made even better progress, and soon she began to talk a few words. Her physical movements which had been awkward and jerky, suddenly loosened up and became co-ordinated, so it was plain that far from being physically handicapped, she was a natural athlete. Mrs Gray's relationship with her became closer than ever before, in spite of the new baby, and Susan would react warmly to her, while she took a real pride in her progress. Finally, Mr Gray once more resumed his more attentive role, provided new carpets for several rooms and began to take his wife out in the evening again.

It would be nice to be able to end this story on such a pleasant note, but more has happened since then. Mrs Gray has had another baby, and at the end of her pregnancy she again became ill and depressed, with similar if less drastic results. Susan had a spell in hospital again, and although she has now reached school age, the authorities have not yet found her a place in a special school or training centre, and there are problems about her continuing to attend the playgroup as they have withdrawn their financial support from this also. As Mrs Gray points out, it is difficult for her not to reject Susan, with all the other demands on her from her other children and with no relief at all from the day-to-day difficulties of caring for Susan in particular. But her relationship with Susan is much stronger now, and whatever happens it seems that there is a bond between them which will survive the ups and downs (which appear to be an inevitable part of Mrs Gray's life) as she grows up and receives her education, and Mrs Gray is aware of her importance to Susan. Her marriage has survived, and as long as she is able to maintain her independence and cheerfulness, her husband treats her quite well, though he cannot be counted on when she is down.

Above all, Mrs Gray still feels the lack of a supportive female relative. She now lives near Mr Gray's family, and has several friends in the street, but none of them can be relied on to take charge of Susan, even though they do sometimes look after the other children. Mrs Gray feels that not having a mother of her own has been her biggest disadvantage during her married life, and I suppose that in my odd way I have tended to adapt my role to try to fit this need, especially in things like taking Susan to the playgroup and taking Mrs Gray shopping. However I have not been successful in helping Mrs Gray to overcome her apparent need to create and recreate situations in which she becomes the underdog, depressed and unable to cope. She has now been sterilised but I have a feeling that some other form of crisis or illness may take the place of pregnancy as the cause of these periodic returns to her Cinderella role.

It is quite probable that if she had had an adequate network of female relatives and friends to help and support her in the problems of bringing up Susan, Mrs Gray would have required nothing of a social worker. As it was, the direct and practical help I was able to give was limited, though I was glad to be able to provide it, and believe it to have been an important part of my relationship with the family. Apart from this, I have noticed a great change in the way in which Mrs Gray talks about Susan over the time I have known her, and I think that I have been of some help to her as she has learnt to relate much better to her daughter, and to offer her much more. When she is well and happy, Mrs Gray no longer fears so much the demands that Susan makes on her, and she misses her whenever she is away from home, but there are still times when she is depressed when her relationship with Susan is felt to be an impossibly demanding one, from which she must escape at all costs.

Similarly, Mr Gray has found that he can be a much better husband, but only when his wife's expectations of him are ones which he feels adequate to meet. He still fears and flees from her depression when things go wrong. As he predicted, the new house has made some difference to their family relationships, and there can be no doubt that the old flat exaggerated the difficulties they were experiencing when I first met them. However, neither the new house nor the practical help I have given them has been sufficient to avoid those moments of crisis when the centrifugal forces in family life have caused a temporary separation of Susan from the rest of the group; nor indeed have my efforts to help them face the emotional issues involved in these crises and separations. However, it was necessary to try to help them face some of these issues as emotional issues, and family issues, simply because they had a way of meeting their needs through external relationships, and I could not meet them myself. It is no good pretending that I could be a one-man female social network, and I suppose what I have tried to provide is a small bit of the practical help that Mrs Gray might have received from such network as part of a social work relationship aimed at helping her overcome her worst feelings about being alone and unsupported. Above all, although at times I have found her depression almost unbearable, and on occasions I have felt very angry with her, I have not allowed her to cause me to reject her and withdraw my help in the way she has caused this to happen periodically in her other relationships in the past; nor have I ever done anything to cause her to believe that I did not think that she was capable, with help, of bringing up her family.

What I am suggesting, therefore, is that the centrifugal tendencies in the Gray family represent an extreme version of a normal pattern of family interaction which depends in large measure for its success on the existence of supportive networks of kin and neighbours. Mrs Gray started by lacking such a network, and the one she has now developed is not adequate to help her with her problems with Susan. A social worker faced with this kind of situation cannot by himself replace this network, or patch up its deficiencies in the way a neighbour or a relative might try to do; still less can he play the kind of role that Mrs Gray's mother, had she been alive and nearby, might most usefully have played. What he can do is to look for practical ways of giving assistance and at the same time offer her a relationship in which she is helped to face the aspects of family life which, without such support, she most fears. This has involved encouraging Mrs Gray to develop a way of feeling about family life, and about Susan in particular, which is at variance with some of the normal patterns and widespread attitudes towards the family of which her centrifugal tendencies represent a rather extreme form. But in the circumstances of Mrs Gray's life, with her whole Cinderella history, this kind of help is the only kind that can be realistically offered. The social worker cannot be a fairy godmother, either in finding a total environmental solution to her day-to-day difficulties, or in offering her a relationship that magically relieves her of all her cares. He can look for ways of meeting her justifiable needs to externalise some of her problems of bringing up Susan, but he cannot enable her to externalise these problems altogether without removing her rights as a parent as well, and thus doing violence to many of her feelings as Susan's mother.

The Murdoch family

Some of the same difficulties were presented by the Murdoch family, a young couple with two children (Brian and Mary) aged six and two. Mr Murdoch was the youngest of four brothers who were known as hard men and heavy drinkers. He had been much affected by the death of his father when he was twelve years old. Although his normal manner was pleasant, slow-spoken and friendly, when he was drunk he was argumentative, aggressive and sometimes violent, especially to his wife. Mrs Murdoch was an illegitimate child whose mother had married when she was seven, and who had felt left out of the family which resulted. Intelligent, sharp-tongued and edgy, she was subject to violent swings of mood, from happiness to bitter anger and finally tears, during which she seemed to switch off one feeling to turn on another.

When I first got to know them they had recently moved to Mrs Murdoch's home town. Their marriage had already been a stormy one and they had had several short separations after violent quarrels. During my first few interviews with them they were concerned about their two-year-old daughter's restless and wakeful behaviour at nights. I guessed that this might be related to quarrels between them, which Mrs Murdoch partially confirmed by saying that when her husband became angry with Mary she found herself secretly hoping that Mary would not give way. Mr and Mrs Murdoch acknowledged that they were both stubborn and obstinate people, and we had begun to discuss their differences in a couple of interviews when I got news that Mr Murdoch had left his wife and returned to live with his mother in his home town, about five miles away.

When I visited Mrs Murdoch, she looked pale but calm. However, as soon as I arrived Mary, who was with her, started to cry, and Mrs Murdoch picked her up and put her on her knee, where she continued to cry. Brian was also in the room looking very sad and Mrs Murdoch told me he had been ill ever since his father had left. However, Mrs Murdoch said with no trace of feeling that she thought it a good thing that he had left. They had been quarrelling ever since my last visit, until finally a physical fight had taken place in which she had been hurt. She had told him to leave and had kept on at him until he went. Mrs Murdoch then suddenly said that she thought that all of their difficulties were basically sexual. He was always pestering her, and she was always fighting him off, which made her feel frigid, even though she was not. He never gave her a chance to respond because he was so aggressively persistent. At other times she found him dull, and was bored in his company. When I remarked that it sounded as if Mrs Murdoch had been finding her husband both annoying and boring, she snapped back at me that I was saying it was her fault. I denied this, but suggested that their quarrels seemed to be a mixture of anger and sadness, and although she was usually the angrier one, it sounded as if she was now feeling very sad about what had happened, and they were all missing Mr Murdoch a lot. At this Mrs Murdoch burst into tears, and at that moment Mary, who had been crying loudly, stopped. Mrs Murdoch said her husband had returned once since leaving, but she had been too frightened of another fight to let him in, and he had not been back since. She felt she could kill him, yet she thought she wanted him more than he wanted her. She feared she brought out the worst in him, as he was only violent with her. I suggested that he was able to make her feel worse than anyone else, as it was only over him that she could feel so sad and miserable. At this she said she never apologised or felt sorry for anything she did, and only recently had had a row with an aunt, but had not taken back a word or felt any regret. We talked about her fear of meeting her husband again, and when I suggested a meeting in my office she seemed to welcome this idea.

After this I contacted my colleague in Mr Murdoch's area, who started to see him regularly, but found him unwilling to meet his wife. Mrs Murdoch reacted to this news by saying angrily that her husband should have Mary with him. When I said I thought it would hurt her a lot to let Mary go, she denied having any real affection for her daughter. She would be happier out at work. I suggested that perhaps there was a boring and depressing aspect of married life that she found hard to bear, and from which she felt she could now escape. At this she said that she really found life very difficult without her husband, and as we talked about this she said she was really very fond of Mary, and wanted him to have her only to remind him of his marriage, which he might otherwise forget. She was very much afraid of him finding another woman, and she blamed herself for their sexual difficulties. She again came near to tears in saying how much she wanted to hold on to her husband, and we talked about how Mary seemed to represent their love for each other, and how because of this she found Mary's presence hard to bear at times. After this interview, Mrs Murdoch wrote me a very depressed letter, saying she could not bear to part with Mary, that she blamed herself for her husband's leaving, and that she felt he was better off without her.

When I next saw Mrs Murdoch, she was even more distressed than before. She said that because Mary had been so ill and pining for her father the previous weekend, she had rung him at work and asked him to visit them. She said that when he came he had been very nice at first, particularly with Mary. However, when he had started to go, she had broken down and begged him to stay; this had led to a row and he had gone off in a temper. She regretted what had happened and thought he might have returned if she had not become so upset, but in another way she said she was glad as it would not have lasted if he had come back. When he had left she had been quite hysterical and had even contemplated suicide. She said she had never previously been lonely in her life, even though she had never got on with her family. At the time she had been in such a bad state that she had gone to see an aunt, who had allowed her to stay for the night, much to her surprise. She had gained something from finding that her family would help her, even when she was as depressed and wild as she had been the previous night. She had never previously had a show of affection from them, and had felt very grateful for the reception they had given her.

Only a week after this interview, Mrs Murdoch rang my office when I was out, threatening to go and kill her husband. I found her actually on her way to his house, and managed to persuade her to return home to discuss what had happened. She was screaming with fury, and repeatedly threatening to murder him. He had again returned, and this time slept with her. There had been no quarrel, and he had left to fetch his clothes back, but had not turned up again. Mrs Murdoch felt utterly humiliated by this treatment, and was determined that he should not get away with it. I talked with her for an hour, but she was still going to go and confront her husband with a weapon. I therefore offered to go and see him for her, and found myself sheepishly knocking on his door, with her and the children in my car some distance up the road. He was surprised but polite, and told me infinitely reasonably that he had been thinking of returning to his wife, but had now changed his mind. He said he had felt confused, and often wanted to see his wife, but was now determined not to return. As there was little more I could say, and I was clearly in a false position being there at all, I had to return to Mrs Murdoch and tell her what had happened. She was furious with me for 'wasting her time', and soon made off after him. She did not succeed in seeing him that evening, but he turned up at her house the following morning. They had another row, she again became hysterical, he hit her, and she returned to her family, who again took her under their wing.

From this description of events over a period of a few weeks it can be seen just how violent were the feelings aroused in both Mr and Mrs Murdoch by their relationship with each other, and just why they had repeatedly escaped from each other by means of brief separations, even before these events took place. Both had had unhappy childhoods for different reasons, Mr Murdoch because of the death of his father, with whom he was very close, and Mrs Murdoch because of her quarrels with her mother. Because of this, both had high expectations of marriage, and invested strong feelings in their relationship, which at times overwhelmed them. While they were together, neither saw much of the families of origin to which they both now turned. Their parents were for both of them a refuge of the last resort rather than a source of continuous support.

The centrifugal tendencies in the Murdoch family, therefore, were generated by moments of crisis in which each partner found the intensity of his feelings unbearable. Their ideal of family life was one in which the emotional satisfactions they could provide for each other were very important, and although they both enjoyed social contacts outside, these were of secondary importance to them. However, such an ideal was seen as unattainable for much of the time, and they lived perilously near to the emotional explosion that they feared might destroy them altogether. The escape of separating was the one way they could find to protect themselves against this; for Mrs Murdoch another way was to turn to me in times of crisis to save her from herself.

Just how this kind of pattern affected their relationships with the children can be seen from the events which followed. After the crisis, Mr Murdoch did not contact his wife for some time, during which she was much calmer. She talked a good deal about the difficulties in their sexual relationship, her feelings about these, and the contribution she made to them. She expressed quite a lot of anxiety about becoming dependent on my visits. She worried that she might be going mad, and asked about seeing a psychiatrist. She became annoyed that her husband did not try to see the children, and a visit by them to his house was arranged. Through this contact with the children he began to visit her again, rather formally, and both took care to be 'nice' to each other. For several weeks these strange polite meetings took place without apparent difficulty, and Mrs Murdoch discussed them and her feelings about them with me. She was pleased that she and her husband could be so pleasant to each other. However, one night he came to the house drunk, she refused to let him in, he broke in, there was a quarrel, and he stopped coming. After a few weeks he came again, but after one reasonable meeting the same thing occurred. After this, Mrs Murdoch decided to see a solicitor about a divorce. Several months went by before he went to see her again, and again they started to have regular meetings.

Soon after this I called to see Mrs Murdoch and found her looking very composed. She had had another quarrel with her husband, and he had gone off in a huff. She said that in any case she was in a mess, having got in arrears with the rent. On top of this she had been being very cruel to Brian and Mary, shouting at them, smacking them and putting them to bed for nothing. She had allowed Brian to stay at home from school in the mornings although he was not ill, mainly because she couldn't get up in the mornings, and at the weekends she just lay in bed and let the children help themselves to food. I said I realised that she was not being as good a mother as she could be, but I did not think that she really wanted to be parted from the children, nor did the children want to be parted from her. Mrs Murdoch denied this, but her tears betrayed her mixed feelings. At this point, Brian returned from school and Mrs Murdoch appealed to him to confirm her stories about herself, that she was a bad mother and that he would rather live elsewhere. I asked Brian what he thought of his mum and he said he thought she was a good mum. Mrs Murdoch, in floods of tears, shouted at him to tell me just how bad she was, and while he confirmed the incidents of harsh punishment which she had listed, he very bravely said that he loved her and that he did not want to go anywhere else, in spite of her appeals and threats to say otherwise. At this point I found myself weeping also. When she saw that Brian would not change his mind, Mrs Murdoch began to talk about her own feelings about her situation. I said I knew how strong these feelings were, as I had been through a situation with her in the past where these feelings were just as strong in her. We talked about this, and how Mrs Murdoch had then feared she was going mad, but would not have thanked me for calling in a psychiatrist as things later turned out. I suggested that at such times she wanted to escape from her own feelings, and tended to see the cause of these feelings as outside herself, in her husband, for instance, or her children. I strongly suggested that it was from her feelings and not from her children that she wanted relief. We talked about her need for help, and how difficult she found it to ask for this, especially from her parents and family, because of her independence. I said I was well aware of how much she needed help now, and arranged to see her again the following day.

When I called the next day, Mrs Murdoch was looking after the child of one of her friends as well as Mary. She envied her friend's freedom, but said she would never let anyone else look after Mary, as it would upset her. When I drew attention to what Mrs Murdoch was saying, she insisted that there was no contradiction here because she was convinced that if she disappeared altogether the children would grieve at first, but soon get over it and forget her when they appreciated the better life they would have. She said that she had in no way changed her mind, and was still determined that the children should be received into care. As we discussed this she started to talk about her own childhood. She said that because she was illegitimate her mother had had to go out to work, and she had been brought up by an aunt who was strict, fair and utterly unfeeling. She remembered clinging to her mother and begging her not to go to work, and she remembered wetting the bed in the early morning to try to get her mother to pay her more attention before she went. She also remembered her mother having another illegitimate baby when she was just starting school, and quite cheerfully having this child adopted. Her mother had married when she was nine, and when she had quickly had two children by this marriage, she had left them in her daughter's care most of the time while she went out in the evenings. Her mother's whole life seemed to have been based on an escape from her feelings, leaving the child to carry all the depression and anger (and much of the responsibility). Mrs Murdoch thought that she had felt more strongly about the adoption of the illegitimate baby than her mother had. We talked about the very different sort of mother that Mrs Murdoch had been to her children, protecting them from painful separations, and as much as possible from the turmoil of family conflict. I realised that she now felt she was doing what was best for them by asking for them to be removed, though I stated quite bluntly that I knew it was not best. On the other hand, I said I realised that she could not be expected to continue to feel as bad as she did and to have to care for them unaided. Mrs Murdoch was angry at my refusal to act directly on her request for the children to be received into care, but I promised I would inform the Children's Department of all her complaints about herself, and they would take action if they thought it appropriate.

I was quite anxious about the situation when I talked to the Children's Department, but they encouraged me to continue to try to avoid the children's reception into care. I was saved from further anxiety when I visited a couple of days later to find that Mrs Murdoch was very relieved that no action had been taken, because her husband had returned to live with her.

It is worth stopping at this point in the story to consider what happened during these few days, for this illustrates very clearly one of the most uncomfortable roles that a social worker can be given. Mrs Murdoch was here trying hard to externalise the unbearably intense feelings that had been caused in her by yet another painful breakdown of an attempted reconciliation. The means of externalising these feelings was myself as a social worker. She found the children unbearable because they reminded her of her feelings about her husband that she was trying to deny, but also because she cared very much about them herself. They also represented the day-to-day demands made on her which in her state of depression she felt unable to meet. She knew I cared about the children, and she was able to use me to relieve herself of having to feel for them. She insisted that she be allowed to escape from them and the feelings they represented, and she could do this through me. She threatened me with all her irrationality and violence, and she succeeded in frightening me a good deal. I really did lose some sleep those few nights thinking what might happen to those children, knowing just how wild and violent she could be. Yet to have removed the children at her request would simply have confirmed all her worst fears about herself. Once separated from them she might never have been able to trust herself to have them back again. In this situation, it was only the knowledge of her gained by having seen her through the earlier, equally frightening, crisis with her husband that gave me the

93

courage to withstand the very strong pressure she put on me to take the children away from her. I hope that in both these crises, the fact that my actions told her that she was neither mad nor a potential murderer of her children (both of which she greatly feared she was) helped her gain some strength and a greater faith in her inner resources to resist the emotions which threatened to overwhelm her.

Mrs Murdoch was a very difficult person to help for many reasons. Her childhood experiences had left her with strong feelings and violent means of dealing with them (mainly by denial and transmission to others) which were not very effective. She was stubborn and independent, and found it difficult to use any help she might have got from her mother's family, though there are some doubts how effective this would have been, except in an absolute emergency. But above all she tended to alternate between strongly denying that she needed help, or that she had feelings about her situation, and equally strongly seeking protection through me from the very strong feelings which welled up in her. She felt her own control over these feelings to be so weak that she fought to get these outside herself, and to have them controlled by external forces. The form which this took—of demanding the separation of the children from her—was quite unacceptable because of its implications both for them and for herself, and my aim was therefore to help her to face her feelings as within herself, and to discover they were not quite as dangerous as she feared.

The rest of the story can be quite shortly told. Mr and Mrs Murdoch lived fairly happily together, with some ups and downs, for a further few months. Unhappily, however, Mrs Murdoch had allowed rent arrears to build up while her husband was away, and this issue became the focus of their negative feelings towards each other. I found myself fighting their battle against eviction (to the point of being reprimanded by the county court judge), while the two of them fought each other rather than for themselves. Mrs Murdoch seemed to feel that she deserved to be evicted, that Part III accommodation was a kind of prison sentence that she had earned, that it would do her good, and that she would be able to cope with it better without any connection with her husband. She also seemed to see it as a place in which her feelings could be kept under control, and she even welcomed the idea of supervision. Mr Murdoch alternated between a bland denial of the problem, and furiously blaming his wife for it. In spite of my efforts to help them, they failed to take any steps to pay any of the arrears or to find alternative accommodation, and split up just before the eviction took place. Mrs Murdoch went into Part III accommodation with the children, and after I had visited her there a couple of times she asked me not to come again, as I reminded her of painful feelings about her husband. I continued to see him for some time afterwards (he was living with his mother), but although he started to visit his wife again, he preferred not to discuss this, and eventually broke off contact with me.

About two years later I saw Mrs Murdoch again by chance. She had returned with the children to her home town, where she had been given a council house. It had been made a condition for this that she should divorce her husband, something which she had resisted doing for quite a long time. The children were very well, and they seemed a very happy family group together. Not long after this, Mrs Murdoch remarried.

Just before Mrs Murdoch went into Part III accommodation she told me accusingly that I had always been trying to reconcile her with her husband, and that I had been very pleased when they had been reconciled for a time. I strongly denied this, and when she reduced this accusation to the suggestion that I looked happy when they were reconciled, I pointed out that she did too. It was certainly true that during the time I had known her I had come to be very closely connected with her feelings about her husband, and her doubts about the possibility of living with someone she loved, or living without him. I very much hoped that she could discover that it was possible for her to love someone without this arousing in her other powerful feelings which threatened to destroy her. In the end she was never able to find a way of living with her husband, but she did succeed in overcoming her great fears about herself as a mother to her children, and they seem to have benefited as much as she has from this experience. Thus it was possible, by turning her in the direction of her own emotional resources at a time of acute crisis, to help her achieve a better solution than the one she was trying to bring about.

The Horn family

I shall now return to the Horn family, mentioned in the last chapter, who provide another illustration of a family in an emotional crisis using a social worker to externalise an emotional problem. Mr and Mrs Horn had long-standing difficulties in their relationship, which had led to their separating, but the reason for my involvement with the family was the non-attendance at school of their son Norman (aged twelve). In the last chapter I described how, after a series of stormy scenes (in which his mother repeatedly threatened to leave the family), Norman began to attend school again. I visited the home weekly after this, but after a couple of weeks Norman missed several days' school, and only returned when I threatened to take him back to court. When we discussed the difficulties in getting him off in the morning, Mr Horn hinted that his wife tended to magnify these by picking a tremendous fight with him if he was at all reluctant to go, provoking him to anger and violence by the things she said to him. When I next visited the house, Norman had again missed a day's school, and Mrs Horn complained bitterly of the trouble he caused, saying she had had enough of fighting to get him to go to school. After a few words with Norman, I spoke to Mr and Mrs Horn who had gone into another room. I pointed out that Norman's failure to go to school seemed to be tied up with fighting with his mother. At this there was a loud shout from another adjoining room (the door was shut, but it obviously came from Norman's seventeen-year-old brother, Frank) that I did not know anything about the fighting that went on in the family. Mr Horn shouted back at Frank to shut up, but Frank continued to shout that I should know about some of the things that went on. I tried to bring Frank into the room by saying very loudly that I could see there was a lot of fighting in the family, and this encouraged him, still from behind the closed door, to elaborate further about fights between himself and his father. I eventually asked him why he did not come into the room, at which he said he would and did. At this point, Norman started to come into the room from the other direction, and both Frank and Mr Horn immediately chased him out. I asked why Norman should not come in, and after some consideration they allowed him to do so. Mr Horn and Frank then started going hammer and tongs at each other, shouting at the tops of their voices, Frank accusing his father of starting any number of fights with him and his mother, particularly through his insane jealousy, and accusing her of having affairs with other men. Mr Horn insisted that his wife was now a very good woman, and particularly a wonderful mother to the children, more or less implying that this was in spite of what she might have been before. I said I didn't accept Mr Horn's version of what his wife had been in the past, but nor did I think that she was necessarily perfect in every way as a mother nowadays as he was claiming. Mr Horn and Frank both rounded on me in defence of Mrs Horn, but she herself volunteered the information that she was often bad-tempered and particularly that she picked fights with Norman. I suggested that these fights with Norman, which she was asking me for help over, were really just part of a wider pattern of fighting in the family. They all tended to deny this, but at once the parents started to argue with Frank about his failure to pay his lodge money. When we had discussed this rather more reasonably, and Frank seemed about to agree with his parents on this point, his father burst out, quite out of the blue, 'Anyway, my word is law, and from now on you will pay an extra ten shillings per week or get out.' Once more a torrent of anger engulfed the family, before I was able to point out how Mr Horn seemed to invite rejection and isolation by the way he had put his view.

When I visited the next week Norman had not missed any school, but the following week I was called out by the family between visits, to be told by Mrs Horn of another row between her and Norman. At this I injudiciously suggested that I would rather discuss this on my next regular visit to the home. When this came, I received a very angry reception from the whole family. Norman hid from me and refused to go to school any more; Mrs Horn said she would have no more to do with getting him there, and that he could go away for all she cared, and she shouted from another room that if I wasn't interested there was no point in my coming. Mr Horn said nothing much except that it was not his wife's fault. After this highly unsuccessful visit, I arranged for Norman to reappear in court, where he was committed to a remand home for three weeks. Norman went wild, burst into tears, and wailed, 'But Mum won't like it.'

I had resolved that I would try to use the three weeks mainly in discussing with Mrs Horn the feelings which lay behind her fights with Norman and with her husband, and which made it so hard for the family to get on with each other. I knew that Mrs Horn would talk very rejectingly about all her family, especially Norman, just as she always did in front of them, but I thought I might be able to reach the well-concealed feelings of love that she clearly had for them all, which she was so afraid of showing, and of which Norman in particular was so much in need. If she could allow herself to experience and to express some of these feelings, I thought the whole atmosphere in the family might begin to change.

When I first saw her after the court (which she did not attend), I said I knew she must be very upset, and I thought for one moment that she was going to cry. Instead she fought this off, and for the rest of the interview expressed the very hardest attitudes. Norman deserved to be put away, and it would do him some good. She would have nothing to do with him while he was there. After talking like this for a while, she suddenly said, 'I suppose it's all because I hate the old man so much', but went on to justify this hatred of him and the children in terms of the bad treatment she received from all of them. She was just an unpaid servant, and all women must feel as she did if they were honest enough to say so. She acknowledged that her life had been particularly unhappy because of her childhood in the home, but insisted that the better care she tried to give the children was simply out of a sense of duty, and because there was no escape from them anyway. She felt no love, and saw happiness only in terms of freedom, though she hardly knew what she meant by this, never having had it. Later on she talked about how Norman would behave better at the remand home because he was more restricted. I suggested that if Norman's mad and wild behaviour at home was the result of freedom, perhaps for her freedom was the equivalent of wildness and madness.

My second interview with Mrs Horn started in the same entirely negative vein, but during the latter part of it there were definite signs of a change. When she talked of her unwillingness to visit Norman, she acknowledged that she was very afraid that she would become upset when she saw him, and that she, like him, was 'very emotional'. We were able to talk about this side of her personality, how well she concealed it, and how vulnerable she felt about it, and I related this to her early experiences. In the meantime, she had also written to Norman. In my third interview, with her and her husband, we talked about how much Norman missed home (he was frequently in tears at the remand home) whereas he behaved so angrily, especially towards his mother, when he was with them. I slowly worked towards the position where I suggested that some of the things which Mrs Horn said to him made it sound as if she might leave him, or leave the family, and that this might give him a sense of insecurity and make him afraid of going to school. She seemed to listen quite carefully to what I was saying, and discussed it calmly with me. I made it clear that I wanted Norman to return home at the end of the three weeks, and by the next interview both Mr and Mrs Horn were able to express the feeling of looking forward to having him back. He duly returned, and since then has gone to school regularly. Since then there has been a great improvement in the whole atmosphere of the family, and I have only on two occasions in the last two years seen any evidence of the kind of conflict that was taking place before this crisis.

In the Horn family, Norman was the member who most expressed the family members' need for and dependence on each other, and who made the greatest emotional demands on his mother. But because of her own child-hood deprivation, Mrs Horn felt that to love and be loved was dangerous and likely to prove hurtful. Through a long and complicated manoeuvre, involving the whole his-tory of non-attendance at school, Norman was eventually removed from the family through my action (his removal had been recommended by the child guidance clinic before I ever came on the scene). It was only after I had thus been forced to collude with her need to separate Norman off from the family that it was possible to help Mrs Horn to allow herself to express something of what she really felt for Norman and the rest of the family, with encourag-ing results.

Before this time, as a result of her own childhood ex-periences, she had seen the role of the social worker purely in terms of punishment and taking members of the family (especially children) away from home. In spite of my efforts to avoid this role, I was eventually forced to play it in relation to Norman, and thus to collude with the centrifugal, splitting off tendency of the family. However, because I had sensed something of Mrs Horn's secret feelings of affection and concern for her family, I did not allow this considerable setback to put me off my aim of helping her to find a more overt expression of what was concealed beneath her harsh and rejecting words. Once again, it eventually proved possible to help the family find greater strength in their own resources than they had thought existed.

People like Mrs Horn and Mrs Murdoch would probably be described in casework literature as 'immature' or 'impulsive'. Writers like Hollis might comment on their faulty ego-functioning and poor impulse control.[4] But to try to understand their behaviour in terms of individual psychological mechanisms is really to misunderstand its basis. Such people flee from the very strong feelings generated by family life, and seek to deal with them in external relationships, either by passing them on to somebody else (transmission) or else by getting themselves into relationships and situations in which these feelings are controlled by the actions of other people.

We may understand more about these patterns of behaviour by starting from the sociological studies of the patterns of family life in which family members are characteristically involved in close-knit social networks outside the nuclear family group. It appears that in such families the norms governing the behaviour of the parents are to a considerable extent determined by these networks, and that, particularly on the mother's side through her female kin, members of these networks play an important part in the upbringing of children. Thus the socialisation of children consists less of the internalisation of the standards of behaviour of two all-powerful parents, than of a system of external controls on behaviour provided by a number of people outside the nuclear family, as well as by the parents. On the father's side, working-class authoritarian patterns, which reinforce the tendency in children to see control as external, are themselves often related to the wider social context of the adult male's position, where a workman is expected to take orders rather than to be responsible for what he does.[5] Thus how people deal with their feelings, and particularly how they control them, must be closely related to the social determinants of their family's pattern of life. There is reason to suppose that the concept of an all-powerful ego, which governs all the norms of social conduct, is the product of a pattern of family life in which parents encourage internalisation of their standards. In families where social control is partially exercised from outside the nuclear family, emotional problems are likely to be taken outside the family group to members of a social network, or failing that to an official such as a social worker, in the expectation that a clear-cut authoritative answer can be provided to a problem which has become clouded in emotional confusion.[6] It may be this difference in family patterns, rather than any emotional 'deficiencies' that explains the different reactions to social workers encountered in people with very different social backgrounds.

However, for people who have lacked both the support of a strong family group and of a social network, social workers and other official authority figures may come to provide the same kind of external system of controls at some period in their lives. Such was the case from her earliest childhood with Mrs Horn; the same thing occurred to Mrs Gray during her adolescence. This way of dealing with feelings is much less satisfactory, both because of the extreme rigidity of the mostly closed institutions which are connected with the official system of controls over behaviour (approved schools, prisons, mental hospitals, etc.) and also because social workers cannot provide consistent day-to-day support in the way neighbours and relatives can. Thus, for the kind of people discussed in this chapter—members of centrifugal families, who lack the support of an adequate social network—social work has to try to provide a personal service aimed at reducing people's need for the institutionalised safety of hospitals, and prisons. It has to make a simultaneous attempt to give some of the help which is so desperately demanded, along with encouraging the development of such a person's own internal resources to face up to emotional difficulties. In the next chapter I shall provide a longer and more detailed account of such a process.

References

1 J. E. Mayer and N. Timms, *The Client Speaks: Working Class Impressions of Casework*, Routledge & Kegan Paul, 1970.
2 J. Packman, *Child Care: Needs and Numbers*, Allen & Unwin, 1968.
3 *Case Con.*, 1, August 1970.
4 F. Hollis, *Casework: A Psychosocial Therapy*, Random House, 1963.
5 M. Kohn, 'Social class and the parent-child relationship', *American Journal of Sociology*, January 1963.
6 Mayer and Timms, op. cit.

4

Working in family situations

The individual approach to social work had the great advantage of having a clear focus. The social worker could concentrate on the needs of his individual client, and on ensuring that these were met as fully as possible, both by himself and by the other people with whom he came into contact. Thus, while social work focused on the individual, work with his family was aimed simply at trying to get them to behave in ways which would make life better for him.

Once the focus of work becomes the family, its aims and objectives are not nearly so clear. The social worker meets all the members of the family, and recognises their often conflicting needs, and he is unsure where to start. He is tempted to try to be all things to all of them, to offer each of them something in turn, to carry over the individual approach into his relationship with each member of the family.

To attempt to do this is really to miss the whole point of family work, which must take the family as its unit of account. In deciding to work with a family rather than just with an individual, the social worker is recognising that the family functions as a unit in certain important respects, and that the ways in which family members behave towards each other reflect shared attitudes about how they can all pool their resources for their mutual benefit and protection. If there were no such shared family norms and no resulting advantages to family members, then the group would not stay together. By working with members individually in turn without taking account of these common factors, the social worker runs the risk, especially with centrifugal families, of weakening the links between the members of the family on which they all depend for the purposes of their day-to-day lives. Alternatively, and especially in integrative families, he may fail to recognise the extent to which family ties prevent individuals from accomplishing their aspirations outside the family group.

On the other hand, if the worker is to concentrate on the family unit, and on the common interests and shared activities of the group, then he is bound to sacrifice his concern with the needs of individual members to some extent. If he is dealing with what is common to all, with the shared element, then he must neglect what is individual and divergent to some extent. This concern with the shared element in family life seems especially relevant to centrifugal families, who have real difficulties with this aspect of their situation, and who fear the emotional involvement of family life. On the other hand, there is some danger in the same approach with integrative families of colluding with the tendency of the family to frustrate all attempts by individuals to diverge from the family consensus.[1]

However, concern with the family as a unit does not necessarily involve working with the whole family as a group all the time. It is a focus for work, not necessarily a method of working. It simply means that, whatever is being done to try to help any member, the needs of the whole group, and the difficulties that any particular individual has in meeting or reconciling himself with these needs, should be the primary focus. It may often be easier to achieve this kind of family focus by concentrating on an individual member who has particular difficulties in behaving in the way that is required by the rest of the group, in meeting the demands made by family living.

Three examples of this were given in the last chapter.

Mrs Gray, Mrs Murdoch and Mrs Horn all found that family life presented great difficulties, and the problems they had in fulfilling the roles of wife and mother made an important contribution to the difficulties of the family group of which they were part. Two factors in the pattern of their family lives contributed to giving them a key role, and to making this role difficult for them to play. The first was the fact that all three of them had husbands who, to a greater or lesser extent, opted out of responsibility for the bringing up of the children, and took little part in family activities. This was least so of Mr Horn, but it was very much the case with Mr Gray and Mr Murdoch. The second factor was that all three lacked an adequate extended family and social network to support them with their day-to-day difficulties in family life. With Mrs Murdoch this was partly because of her feelings about her family of origin, but the other two had no family to whom to turn. Thus any help that they could be given was important to the family group as a whole.

Although the role of the mother is always both an important and a difficult one in centrifugal families, especially when the age of the children denies her any real escape from the emotional demands of family life, there are some situations in which it seems appropriate to try to work with both husband and wife together as much as possible, and often to include the children as well. Since the time when Norman Horn was in the remand home I have followed this approach with his family, with satisfactory results. I pay weekly visits in which I see as many of the family as are there when I call. One advantage of such a method of working is that it avoids the contrived intensity of the one-to-one interview. If the members of a large family are unaccustomed to the kind of individual relationship with a social worker that this provides, and it makes them uncomfortable, there is often little advantage to be gained in pressing it on them. The exception to this principle in the case of the Horn family was the very emotional situation while Norman was away from home, because his mother had played such an important part in having him removed, and because she was the one member of the family who seemed to be saying that she would prefer not to have him back again. But perhaps more important, seeing the family as a group indicates to them that I see them as a family, and recognise their common interests and needs. Whereas Mr Horn seemed very split off and isolated from the rest when I first started to visit, he is now closely involved in family life, and much more accepted by the rest of the family. On a visit which I made soon after Norman returned home Mr Horn was not in, and the rest of the family started to complain about him, but rather than encourage them to do this I tended to take his part, and show that I respected his point of view. Since then there has been very little evidence of this conflict, and none of conflict between himself and his wife. It might be suggested that the family are now less willing to tell me of such conflict, and this may be the case. However, I could see no great advantage in encouraging them to express these feelings to me, since they had no difficulty in expressing them to each other in the raging battles that had been fought over the years in the family. The help they needed seemed to be more in the direction of finding expression for the affection they felt for each other, and this I seemed to have had some success in doing.

For some time, social work has recognised the special challenge to its claims of professional expertise presented by the 'problem family', the kind of family in which several members' behaviour is simultaneously and variously difficult or 'anti-social', and whose members are often apparently struggling both against each other and against society at large. Where a number of different social problems are found in different members of the same family, it is difficult to see how the family group can be of help to any of its members. The father with a bad work record, the mother a bad housekeeper, the children with various symptoms of maladjustment—what is such a family but the sum total of all its weaknesses? In a problem family it seems that no theory of family interaction is necessary to explain how each member's difficulties are reinforced by the group. It appears only too obvious that 'inadequate' parents will be unable to handle difficult children effectively, and that having several difficult children will undermine such parents and discourage them from making any efforts on their own behalf.

However, I shall try to show that such families require and deserve to be understood in a way which takes account of the strong emotional forces at work within them; that the roles taken by members of such families are not just accidental results of their 'inadequacies', but a reflection of the underlying currents of feeling within the group; and that it may be possible, by working with these strong feelings, to help such families be a source of strength for their members. In other words, although the members of such families do often reinforce each other's weaknesses, it is possible to understand both how and why this occurs through the emotional interaction within the family group, which largely determines the behaviour of each individual within it.

The Sharp family

I shall try to illustrate this from my work with the Sharp family. Mr Sharp had had dealings with two previous social workers from my agency before I got to know him. His age was then thirty-eight. As a very young man he had been married to a woman who humiliated him by her open association with other men during their marriage, before she finally divorced him. He remarried immediately, and his second marriage had been very unsuccessful. He had nothing good to say about his second wife. According to him she was stupid, a bad manager, hopeless with the children, lazy in the house, and above all utterly cold in their sexual relationship. He blamed her for the fact that he had been before the courts on three occasions. Mr Sharp himself seemed intelligent but very evasive and anxious not to reveal too much about himself, so he was very difficult to interview. He had quite a good work record, and was in a semi-skilled job, with an adequate wage.

Mrs Sharp had been well known to the health and education authorities for some time because of her poor management of the home and her difficulties in caring for the children (John, then aged nine, David aged six and James aged four). Her home, which was a post-war council house, was untidy and poorly furnished, and seemed to reflect a good deal of depression. However, she herself was a very angry person, complaining about her husband in tones of bitterness and hatred. She described him as over-sexed, always demanding intercourse, but quite without any affection for her. She said he was critical and bossy, and never even let her manage the house. She wanted nothing so much as to be left entirely alone by him, and often talked of a separation. She had no friends, and seemed to be treated as an outcast in her neighbourhood.

For a time, I saw them both individually, and made no progress either towards understanding or influencing their attitudes towards each other. After a while, I tried to see them together, which seemed quite disastrous. They shouted and swore alarmingly at the tops of their voices for about two hours and I had eventually guiltily to leave them at this, as there was no sign that anything I could say would help them to do anything else. During the next year, Mrs Sharp came to see me on two or three occasions to repeat her complaints about her husband, and tell me that he should be put away. She wanted me to discuss a separation with them, but whenever it came to the point of my seeing Mr Sharp she changed her mind.

Meanwhile, two of the children began to shows signs of disturbed behaviour. John, who had reached the age of eleven, had been referred to the child guidance clinic for soiling, and had been sent to a residential school for educationally subnormal children, thus removing him from the home which was felt to be a bad influence on him. David (eight) was difficult and backward at school, and it was felt that he should eventually follow his brother to the residential school. He was destructive in the home, and banged his head at night. James (six) was quite different; he gave no particular trouble, and was a popular and healthy child.

When Mrs Sharp came to see me yet again, I felt that I had little hope of helping the family. I felt that I had completely failed to be of any help in the past, and I was very gloomy about their future. They made me feel very useless as a social worker, and Mrs Sharp's occasional angry visits to my office always left me depressed. This time, she had her usual complaints about her husband, but the position had slightly changed. She had been seeing another man, and her husband had found out about it. She was thinking of leaving again, but this time with the other man. She said she realised that this was unlikely to solve her problems, and wanted me to call to see her husband to find out whether he really wanted her to stay or not. She said his behaviour had been so bad that she thought he wanted to get rid of her. I agreed to visit them the following week.

When I arrived Mrs Sharp showed me into the sitting-room, where the two younger boys were playing on one side of the room, and Mr Sharp was standing on the other side. The boys started to giggle as soon as I walked in, and Mr Sharp greeted me without enthusiasm. I said I thought he wouldn't be very pleased to see me. He said he couldn't see any reason why he should not be. I said I thought it would make him angry that his wife felt things were bad enough to ask me to come and see them both again. He said he did not realise his wife had asked me to come. When Mrs Sharp challenged this, he said she hadn't spoken to him that evening in any case. If there was anything wrong between them she had not told him about it, and in fact she never told him where he was supposed to have gone wrong. Mrs Sharp said she could not talk to him, he always just slapped her down. She said that only a few weeks ago he had told her he wished he had grounds to divorce her. Mr Sharp tried to dismiss this, saying that she harboured grievances and would not discuss them with him. At this point, Mrs Sharp flared up, and shouted that it was impossible to talk to him. I said I thought she did not talk to her husband because she was afraid she would be criticised, and she said this was perfectly true. Mr Sharp said with an air of injured innocence that he could not remember criticising her, and asked her when he had done so. Mrs Sharp was getting more and more angry, and although she wouldn't give him an example, she called him a liar, and said it was impossible to say anything to him. He said, in a tone of indignation, that the trouble was that she was incapable of talking any sense to him. I said I thought this sounded like a criticism of her. Mrs Sharp then accused him of constantly interfering between her and the children. At this Mr Sharp started to get angry (the boys meanwhile were giggling increasingly loudly, and had stopped playing altogether). He shouted that his wife never got up in time to get the children off to school in the morning. She screamed that he interfered when he did get up. They accused each other of failing to appreciate the efforts each had made. Mr Sharp started to attack his wife for the way she ran the house. She said he took over the house when he was on holiday, refused to speak to her, and told her to shut up when she tried to talk. At this point I said I thought both Mr and Mrs Sharp were convinced that they were unable to be satisfactory as husband and wife to each other. Each was certain that what he or she did would fail to satisfy the other, and that they would be hopeless failures, whatever they tried to do. At this, for the first time, they seemed to pause, and Mr Sharp said he thought there was some truth in what I had said. The children also stopped giggling. Mrs Sharp then said it was their bedtime and took them upstairs (they went without any fuss). Mr Sharp then said that his wife completely rejected any sexual advance he made. She was utterly cold towards him. Mrs Sharp returned, and started saying angrily that she had no feelings for him any more, that he had killed all these by the way he treated her. Very soon they were as angry as before, Mr Sharp accusing his wife of complete coldness and Mrs Sharp saying she wanted nothing more to do with him. I suggested that they were both inwardly afraid of being unable to satisfy each other, both physically and emotionally. Suddenly Mrs Sharp began to tell a story about when they were first married, and as she told it, with tremendous feeling, the tears were running down her cheeks. She said that when they had first been married, on one occasion Mr Sharp had been doing some painting and she suddenly felt she wanted to have intercourse, but that he had rejected her in a brutal way. Mr Sharp looked very anxious about this, and tried to explain that he was doing something very important at the time. I said I felt this was a terribly important turning-point for them. At that time Mrs Sharp had been showing affection and wanting to have intercourse, and her husband was refusing, whereas now it was always Mr Sharp who asked and she who refused. It looked as if he was a very affectionate person and she was not at all, but I did not accept that this was so. I thought Mrs Sharp still had very strong feelings towards her husband, and greatly wanted to return his love, and that Mr Sharp was still rather afraid of his inability to give her sufficient love, and still felt she might demand more than he was able to give. Quite suddenly, from having been quarrelling furiously they fell into a complete silence, which lasted about a minute. Then Mrs Sharp said she thought John understood the situation because he had told Mr Sharp a few home-truths about himself (she had always previously complained that John was entirely on her husband's side, and did nothing but call her horrible names). Mrs Sharp then again mentioned her husband's criticism of her, and I suggested that in everything except sexual matters she tried hard to please him, and that he tended to reject her efforts. When we had discussed this quite calmly for some time, I said that I thought we had made some progress, and that I would like to call again the following week. They both agreed, but as soon as I started to go they began quarrelling furiously again, about fairly small domestic matters. When I was finally able to get a word in, I said I thought they were again expressing their feelings that each of them was hopeless, and they could never satisfy each other. They seemed to accept this, and comparative peace returned before I left.

In this family, both the fights between the parents and their desire to escape from each other seemed to be based on their great hidden fears about themselves in their family roles. One of the things which made Mr and Mrs Sharp so difficult to interview either individually or together, was their anger with each other, and their refusal to see anything other than the terrible shortcomings of the other partner. Although Mr Sharp's anxieties about himself came through in his evasiveness, and Mrs Sharp's depression was shown in her home, they would neither acknowledge these feelings willingly, nor would they look at their own contribution to their marital situation. Their feelings about their own failures as partners and as parents were constantly being denied, and these feelings seemed to contribute to my hopelessness and depression about them. I felt useless and powerless to be of any help to them. I had the feeling that I would never be able to communicate to them any understanding I had of their marriage, and that they were both far too angry and defensive to be able to look at their other feelings. These fears that I had were reinforced by both Mr and Mrs Sharp, and it was not until I drew attention to the feelings that each of them had about their own shortcomings and failures in the marriage that I began to have some hope of helping them, and that they were able to do anything other than shout angrily at each other. Their acceptance of these feelings not only helped them to think about their situation more realistically, but it also relieved me of much of my depression and enabled me to take a more effective part in what was happening.

In this interview, the role of the two boys is also significant. Whenever I had been to the home they had stayed in the room, no matter what was being discussed. Their mother complained to me freely about her husband's sexual behaviour in front of them, and in my one previous joint interview with their parents they had been present for the whole of the furious battle which took place. One could easily surmise that for them fights involving shouting and swearing between their parents were nothing new or surprising. Perhaps to some extent the parents needed them there as a sort of security, so that things were kept within bounds. In particular, they were probably useful when I was there, because they represented another factor making it harder for me to face the parents with their true feelings. Once I had taken a step in the direction of doing this, the children were taken up to bed; it was one thing for them to see their parents fighting, but quite another to glimpse the deeper feelings from which each was trying to escape.

What sort of feelings were these? This first interview gives some clues about the nature of the emotional interaction between Mr and Mrs Sharp. Up till then Mr Sharp had complained of his wife's incompetence, her coldness and her complete lack of feelings for him, while she had portrayed him as over-sexed and domineering. From what they said on this occasion, there was a glimpse of Mr Sharp's uncertainty about his masculinity and of his fears about being unable to satisfy his wife's sexual needs, and also a glimpse of Mrs Sharp as someone who wanted much more from her husband than she cared to admit, a sadder but also a warmer person than she usually made herself out to be. These hitherto unrevealed aspects of their personalities were clearly reflections of feelings about which both had great fears, to the extent that they maintained such deeply unsatisfactory roles towards each other rather than recognise them. Mr Sharp preferred his wife to see him as a bitter, critical, domineering and sexually demanding man rather than allow the weak, anxious and vulnerable aspects of his personality to emerge. Mrs Sharp would rather give the impression of being both incompetent as a housekeeper and cold as a wife than admit that there was a part of her that needed to be loved. For both of them, the behaviour about which they bitterly complained in the other reflected some of the feelings which they could not tolerate within themselves.

In individual interviews Mr Sharp tried hard to give the impression of himself as a reasonable and thoughtful man, who was aware of his situation and attributed his difficulties entirely to his utterly unreasonable wife. Mrs Sharp made no such appeal; she always presented a torrent of angry feelings, as if she wanted to demonstrate that her husband was driving her out of her mind. In the joint interview Mr Sharp started off by trying to maintain his role of a reasonable man, who was just trying to get on with his life in the midst of intolerable provocation from his wife. As usual it was Mrs Sharp who first became wildly angry, and who started to swear and shout. Once the fight began these roles became less distinct, but all the same, there was in this, as in the previous joint interview, a distinct impression that it was Mrs Sharp's anger that might get out of hand and lead to real violence. Even in the most heated quarrel, her husband seemed to be the one who was likely to keep his head. This is important, because throughout everything that happened in my work with this family, the roles which reflected the feelings involved in the interaction were acted out. In the Sharp family, and thus in my work with them, it was not the words which were spoken which indicated the significant events, but the actions of the various people in the situation. The work of helping each of them to accept the feelings which they denied and transmitted to another consisted in their slowly learning to act a slightly different. role, first in interviews and then more consistently within the family. They learnt to tolerate their feelings by experiencing them, and acting them out and finding that they were tolerable to each other also. This took quite a long time.

In this interview, for the first time in the two years I had known the Sharp family, I felt that I was able to begin to be of some help to them. As in the first joint interview I had had with them over a year previously, I was frightened by the intensity of their anger, and there seemed to be something totally incongruous about trying to make comments about what I sensed to be their other well-hidden feelings while they were screaming at each other at the tops of their voices. For one thing, my own remarks had to be made very loudly in order to be heard. I felt like some absurd caricature of a social worker, shouting things about love at these two people who were expressing nothing but hatred towards each other. It was not easy to do that on this occasion, nor was it easy in later interviews, but what I did discover for the first time was that such interventions did make an impact on Mr and Mrs Sharp. For although they both fled from emotional involvement and denied having any feelings invested in their family life, both secretly needed each other very much, and needed help to find some expression and satisfaction of these needs.

The next time I saw them their behaviour contrasted strongly with the anger that they had shown in the first interview. They were cheerful and friendly, and behaved almost flirtatiously towards each other. Mr Sharp made it clear that they were much happier, and that there had been a dramatic improvement in their sexual relationship. However, within a fortnight of this Mrs Sharp was again at my office complaining about her husband, and there was another angry scene when I visited the home. I tried to help them to deal with their disappointment that their 'honeymoon' had not lasted, and there followed an interview in which Mrs Sharp spoke for the first time of her life before her marriage. She said that her family had completely rejected her during her adolescence and that she had been so desperately lonely and depressed at times, that she had thought of committing offences of shopbreaking to try to relieve her feelings. Mr Sharp was evidently shocked by the depth of his wife's feelings of depression as she described this time in her life, and clearly found this hard to tolerate. He tried to reassure her and jolly her out of her depression in a way which showed his fear of it.

In my next interview with them Mr Sharp was playing his role of the reasonable man again, complaining of his wife's impulsiveness and her vindictive behaviour towards him. He contrasted her unfavourably with his first wife, saying that she had a far better way of behaving towards him. When I suggested that in fact Mr Sharp had often been very angry with his first wife; he denied this blandly, saying they had always been on the best of terms. I tried to make it clear that I did not accept this, and that I saw Mr Sharp as having had problems in his sexual relationship with both his first and his second wife. Mrs Sharp also tried to give me the impression that she had been a very docile person before her marriage, and had got on well with everybody, but I tried to indicate that I felt that she, like her husband, had carried over a lot of anger arising from earlier relationships into her marriage.

It was not until the next time I saw them that Mr and Mrs Sharp returned specifically to the problems in their sexual relationship. This time they were very much calmer than in my first interview with them. Mrs Sharp again told me the same story about her husband's refusal to have intercourse with her early in their marriage, but with less emotion, and it provoked less guilt from him. Mr Sharp acknowledged that he might have damaged their relationship by his behaviour then. Mrs Sharp suddenly said that she felt like a servant in her house, and that all she did was work there. This was in fact exactly what she had been doing as a job before her marriage, and I reminded her of this, suggesting that perhaps she had had high expectations of marriage which had been disappointed. Mr Sharp said that this was so, and that she had thought marriage would be a bed of roses. We started to discuss his expectation of marriage, and he agreed that he had no such high hopes because of his experiences in his first marriage. He said that he had been determined not to be hurt a second time. He still claimed that all that was needed was for his wife to make an effort to improve their sexual relationship. I drew attention to Mr Sharp's fears of being hurt by his wife, and suggested that this could include a fear that he might fail to answer her sexual needs in the way which seemed to have happened in his first marriage. Mr Sharp did not really acknowledge this, and before I left he and his wife started to quarrel angrily again, about her housekeeping. I again acknowledged their feelings of hopelessness about their situation, and their need to draw my attention to these before I left.

Up to this point, the main indications that something was happening to the emotional interaction within the family had been an increased willingness on the part of both Mr and Mrs Sharp to look at some of the feelings which they had brought with them into their marriage. Mrs Sharp's ability to tolerate her own depression had been almost matched by Mr Sharp's acknowledgment of some of his anxieties over his sexual role. Furthermore, they no longer seemed to need to involve the children in interviews. Perhaps at this point it might have seemed that the Sharps were beginning to learn to benefit from interviews simply by a slow acceptance of the feelings which they had been denying. However, this was not at all the case, and there was still to be a great deal of dramatic acting out before they could take on roles which were really different from the ones in which they had found some security from their unwanted feelings. This was also to involve the family as a whole, and not just Mr and Mrs Sharp.

On my next visit, Mrs Sharp started by announcing that

she had got herself a living-in job as a chambermaid in a hotel. She said that she had been to see the authorities about arrangements for the children to be looked after. Mr Sharp said that he was not angry about this, and that he could look after the children quite easily. He was determined that no one else should have them. He made it plain that he was not going to give up his family and his home for a second time, and he drew attention to the fact that he was decorating the house, which in fact looked quite a bit better. I said I thought Mrs Sharp also wanted to make a success of her marriage, and wanted her husband to love her. She said that on the contrary, she just wanted to get away from her husband, and thought she would be happier in a job. I suggested that she seemed to be going back to the same sort of life which she had had before her marriage, and in which she had been unhappy. Mr Sharp asked me not to put his wife off if she wanted to go, but to let her try it if that was what she wanted—he implied that she would soon learn her mistake. Mrs Sharp then told me angrily that she had just let her husband know that she had been stealing money from him for a long time. She had been taking the money from a box in which he was trying to save up for a camera. After we had talked about this for a bit, I suggested that Mrs Sharp had partly wanted to get something from her husband which he was keeping from her, like his love, and that in the same way Mr Sharp liked to save up love for himself rather than share it with his wife. Mrs Sharp asked quite seriously whether I really believed that she loved her husband. I said I did, and that I thought one reason why she was thinking of running away was her fear of committing herself to loving her husband. One reason why Mr Sharp would rather let her go than stop her was that he too had fears that she might do this. At this point Mrs Sharp took the children, who had been in the room, up to bed, and while she was upstairs Mr Sharp talked in a depressed way about how miserable his life was, and how his wife never talked to him. Mrs Sharp returned, and said that her husband was not interested in her or her feelings. He did not want to know anything about her. We talked about his fear of the strength of his wife's feelings, and particularly her depression, and her fear that her husband could not possibly love her because she was so bad. She said that she had been very surprised to be accepted for the job, but that she had been determined to try, just to show her husband. Mr Sharp tried hard to deny resentment about his wife's action, but clearly showed his anxiety about her becoming more independent and capable. When he came nearer to acknowledging this, I suggested that he feared she might become too independent, like his first wife. Before I left, Mr Sharp criticised his wife for never offering me a cup of tea. I said I thought the reason why she failed to do this was a feeling that I would not like it or accept it. She said she would make sure I got one next time.

They both remembered the offer of a cup of tea when I next visited the house, but it was Mr Sharp who eventually made it, while Mrs Sharp wandered around rather aimlessly. When the pot was ready Mr Sharp poured the tea in an odd, jerky way, stopping and starting three or four times before filling the cup, and remarking how weak it was. Mrs Sharp was quiet and depressed. She said she had not taken the job because of the school holidays. For the first time, they both began to speak seriously about the children. Mrs Sharp said that the second boy, David, was becoming as bad as John, the eldest. She described his destructive behaviour, telling me how he had got hold of some of his father's most precious possessions and wrecked them. It seemed that most of David's aggression was directed at his father, and Mr Sharp said that he took after his mother. By contrast John, who was closest to his father, was always provoking his mother, both by his soiling and by shouting and swearing at her. It certainly appeared from this interview that David's demanding and destructive behaviour, directed at his father, closely reflected many of his mother's feelings, while John's messy aggressiveness towards his mother was reinforced by the feelings which Mr Sharp, the reasonable man, had to deny.

When I arrived for my next visit, Mr and Mrs Sharp were in the sitting-room with the three boys. John and David had been on holiday and were going back to school the following day. Mrs Sharp looked quite distraught and was flitting about the room. I commented on this, and she told me she was absolutely fed up and going to leave the following day. She said she was sick of having the kids at home with their filthy talk and calling her names all day, and then her husband coming home and telling her filthy stories about women. If he thought so little of women he should never have got married. Mr Sharp complained angrily about his wife, saying that she would not talk to him at all, and that if he approached her she pushed him away. On top of this she was swearing at the children, and their bad language was only picked up from her. Mrs Sharp said that the children told him lies about her and he believed everything they said and just criticised from the moment he came in. I said I thought Mr Sharp's criticisms made her all the more angry because she felt a very bad sort of person, particularly about her difficulties in coping with the children. I then took up with Mr Sharp his criticisms of his wife, and said I thought he needed to believe that he was better than his wife in looking after the children, and to blame her for what went wrong with them rather than to see himself as a bad father. I thought the children told him what he wanted to hear about his wife. Mr Sharp said his wife could not even make a bed properly, and this goaded her to greater fury as she said that she had been in service for many years before marriage and had always given satisfaction. As they started to quarrel about the bed, Mrs Sharp suddenly got quite uncontrollably angry and rushed into the kitchen. Mr Sharp sat absolutely still and apparently calm while she banged and crashed around on the other side of the door, screaming abuse, for several minutes. I was really frightened, as although

I had often seen her very angry, I had never been there when she had lost control so completely. After a while I managed to say very loudly that I thought when there were difficulties between them they always managed to make it look as if Mrs Sharp was the bad and mad one, while Mr Sharp was calm and reasonable, but I did not accept this and thought a lot of the anger and wildness was in Mr Sharp. At this Mrs Sharp burst back through the door with a key, and went and unlocked a cupboard. She asked if she would have to cut her wrists in front of him to make him take some notice. She rummaged around, but eventually said she could not find a razor blade, and came back to her chair, where she picked up a large knife which she brandished at him and at her wrists. It was very difficult for me not to react to this, but I felt to do so would have been to show that I did not really believe the things I said to them about their relationship. I said I thought they were both trying to show me just how desperate things had been in the rather long time since I had last visited. I thought that Mrs Sharp wanted to prove that her life was quite intolerable. Although she went on waving the knife about for a time, she became more tearful and less angry. She repeated that she wanted to get right away and have nothing more to do with any of them. I said I thought she really wanted affection from her husband and children, but did not dare ask for it. She felt she could not trust any show of affection from Mr Sharp and that he would soon turn against her cruelly again. Mr Sharp seemed to be being prevented from being affectionate by his wife, but I thought that there was some hostility towards her even without this rejection. Mrs Sharp talked about how hurt she was by his criticisms, and asked him why he had never criticised or interfered in the early part of their married life, when John was a baby. She could have done with some help from him then, but he had always left her alone. He made the excuse that anybody could manage with one baby, and that in fact babies were easier to manage than older children. I suggested that the pattern of their marriage had been very different at that stage. I thought that Mr Sharp had been afraid of becoming involved with his wife, and of Mrs Sharp demanding too much of him. We returned again to the incident when he had refused to have intercourse with her, and to my suggestion in my earlier interview that this was something to do with his having been hurt by his first wife. Mrs Sharp said he had always wanted her to be more like his first wife. Mr Sharp then suddenly started to tell me for the first time just how badly his first wife had hurt him. He talked of her flagrant infidelity, how she had even committed adultery with his father, and how he had once tried to shoot her. Mrs Sharp constantly interrupted and contradicted him, trying to make out that each incident was either being distorted or invented by him; or else, if true, then his fault. I suggested that Mrs Sharp could not accept that Mr Sharp had been a victim in his first marriage, but felt he must have been the one who hurt and destroyed his first wife. She seemed to have to see him as the destructive one. Mr Sharp confirmed that he had been the victim, and said that Mrs Sharp got a false version of their marriage by writing to his first wife, and had always believed it. I suggested that perhaps he had been as young and innocent when he first married as Mrs Sharp when she married him. He confirmed this, and I went on to suggest that there was still part of him which he felt to be weak and liable to be hurt, but he fought against this happening in his second marriage by dominating his wife and making sure he always kept on top. When we had talked about this for a time, Mr Sharp suddenly said that it was really always the children's fault when they had a row, and told John off for telling lies about his mother. I suggested that both Mr and Mrs Sharp tended to look for one person to be the cause and in the wrong when there were family difficulties, rather than to acknowledge the deep feelings which they both had as a result of being hurt in the past.

When we had discussed this I started to go, and as I did so Mrs Sharp announced that she would still be leaving the following day. I said I thought she wanted me to realise just how difficult things still were; at this she started mentioning other problems as I got to the door. I said I knew she felt I still didn't understand how bad it was, but I would be coming again in a fortnight.

In this interview I was really put to the test by Mr and Mrs Sharp. It was hard enough to say things about their loving each other when they were screaming hatred, but the real question was whether I could act as if I really believed what I said. When Mrs Sharp lost control, could I still continue to see her as a woman who loved and needed love, or would I reveal that I really saw her as a dangerous maniac? When Mr Sharp sat there, apparently unmoved by her outburst, would I continue to treat him as a feeling person, who was involved with his wife and her anger, or would I finally collude with his cold, rational vision of himself? I can still remember vividly how, at the moment when Mrs Sharp was breaking up the kitchen, I took my hand off the table on which it had been resting, and saw that it had left a pool of sweat on the unpolished surface. Those few minutes gave me one of my most frightening experiences as a social worker, but I believe that my reactions were of great importance in helping Mr and Mrs Sharp to discover that the roles they had been playing towards each other were not the only possible ones open to them.

When Mr and Mrs Sharp began to recognise the feelings that they had been denying for so long, the consequent changes in their relationship were quite alarming for them. Just before I was due to visit them, a fortnight after the interview last quoted, I heard that they had had a great row, and Mrs Sharp had left. However, when I visited as arranged I found them at home, both looking a good deal more composed and assured than at the start of the previous interview. Mrs Sharp told me that she had gone away, but had come back because the place where she had gone to work had been too disorganised. Otherwise she would have stayed there. She was very vague about the chronology of what had happened, but I gathered that she had got the job at least ten days previously, and told her husband she was leaving him then. However, it wasn't until the day before that she had actually gone. I said I expected Mr Sharp to tell me that he had not minded his wife going or worried about her coming back. He contradicted this, saying he was very sorry to see her go, and pleased to have her back. He said this with unusual firmness. I asked what led to her eventually leaving, and Mr Sharp became quite anxious at this. He said he could not see the point of dragging it all up again. They were getting on better now, and wanted to forget it. At this point the boys appeared at the door from the other room, and hung about for several minutes while their parents unsuccessfully shouted at them to go away. I said I thought the whole family was rather anxious about talking about what had happened the previous day. It sounded to me as if Mr Sharp had got very angry. He denied this, but said he had got very upset. I said I wondered if he had got so upset that he almost got out of control. He did not deny this, saying that his wife had gone on about leaving so much, and had even been packing her things, that eventually he went for her, told her to get out of the house, and more or less threw her out. I suggested that this was quite frightening for both of them, because it was usually Mrs Sharp who got angry and out of control, as she had done the last time I was there, whereas Mr Sharp was usually calm and calculating. We talked about this, and I suggested that Mrs Sharp had been surprised at her husband's violence in throwing her out, and also that he had welcomed her back when she returned the same evening. She said that all he had done when she returned was to say that it was her fault in the first place. She told me she had been to see her sister, and had had a talk with her eighteen-year-old nephew, who told her that she was neurotic and ought to put up with things more. Then he had brought her back to her husband. Mr Sharp said he had been furious to have a mere boy poking his nose in their marriage, and telling him what to do. I suggested that Mrs Sharp might have been as angry about what was said to her, because it was not nice to be told one was neurotic. Mrs Sharp denied any anger about this. Mr Sharp said that in the end her nephew had come round to his side, saying that he was really in the right. His wife was definitely neurotic, and he defined this as being unable to control her temper. I took up the sort of things that had been said by the nephew, and said that in some ways they were reassuring for Mr and Mrs Sharp because they took them back to their previous situation. He had managed to tell them that Mr Sharp was really calm and reasonable, even though a few hours previously he had been very angry and violent, and that Mrs Sharp was out of control and angry, even though for the previous ten days she had calmly and calculatingly teased Mr Sharp about going away. Now she was seen as the unreasonable one again, and he as the sensible one. When we had discussed this, I suggested that they had been told what they wanted to hear, because what frightened them was being the opposite for a short time. Mr Sharp admitted that he had got terribly angry, and had threatened to murder his wife. Mrs Sharp said she had certainly put off going for a long time, but denied that this was calculated. Both were able to look at this quite calmly, and even smiled about it, though I said I knew it was frightening for them to think that they could be so much the opposite of their normal selves. Mrs Sharp then told me she was starting a part-time job on Monday. Mr Sharp said that the whole trouble had been that she was not like other women; she confined herself to the house and complained about it. I suggested that it was rather frightening for them both to think she might change so much as to have a job. Just as I was going, Mr and Mrs Sharp remarked that the children were now playing quite happily in the garden. I suggested that when they were anxious about what was being discussed or what might be, the children seemed always to be around and interrupting the discussion.

This was the start of the real change in the emotional interaction in the Sharp family. When I next went to the house things seemed very different. Mrs Sharp looked very smart, greeted me cheerfully and said she supposed she had better go and make me a cup of tea. She proceeded to do this very efficiently. Mr Sharp was quiet and looked gloomy, and for once he did not try to make pleasant reasonable conversation with me at the start of an interview. Mrs Sharp told me that she had started work for some old ladies, and the only trouble with it was that they tended to talk rather a lot and hold her up from her work. Apart from this she was quite satisfied, and they seemed to be also. She said once they had kept her late, so she had been late getting her husband's meal and he had been in a terrible temper about it. Mr Sharp tried to deny this, and equally my suggestion that it was annoying and inconvenient for him to have his wife working. Mrs Sharp remained very good humoured, and instead of starting an argument with her husband said that he would just have to take his turn. While he still insisted that he was quite happy about his wife working, Mr Sharp said that of course she would have to stop work in the holidays or if the children were ill. Mrs Sharp again did not rise to this, saying simply that there were plenty of other jobs she could get after she had to finish this one when the next school holidays came. We continued to discuss this for a time, and then Mrs Sharp asked me if I agreed with her nephew that she was 'neurotic'. I again said I thought that the incident to which she had referred had shown that her husband as well as she could be angry and uncontrollable. She then said that there were times when she could be calm and work things out quite carefully.

Here Mrs Sharp was acting an entirely new role in the family, and testing out whether her husband and she could tolerate it. She had risked trying to get a job; she had made a bid for the independence that she was neither sure that she wanted, nor that she could attain. In finding out that she could achieve some of these things she no longer had to say that she cared nothing for her children; she was prepared to give up her job in the holidays. She was no longer so sensitive to her husband's criticisms, but she did not have to pretend that she had no wish at all to be a good wife. All this depended to a considerable extent on the fact that Mr Sharp had begun to accept some of the feelings which he had for so long forced his wife to carry for him. Without abandoning his role of reasonable man completely, he was beginning to recognise some of the feelings which contributed both to his wife's violence and incompetence, and to John's aggressive behaviour towards her. But there was to be one more violent crisis before these new roles could be firmly established.

As I was going to see the Sharps for my next visit, I saw Mrs Sharp walking up the road and gave her a lift. She told me that she had been furious with her husband because she had found a pornographic photograph among his possessions. She had been to various people, including the police, about this, but they had all said that they could do nothing about it. When we got to the house Mr Sharp was affable and chatty, seeming anxious to please me. Almost immediately, Mrs Sharp remarked about the photograph. He reacted very angrily, saying that all he had done was to print it for a man at work, not knowing what it was when the negative was given to him. As they began to argue about this, Mr Sharp suddenly flew into a rage, rushed across the room and grabbed his wife by the throat. Having shaken her once or twice, he returned to his side of the room. He sat down gloomily, and I said that I realised how angry he was with his wife for telling me about this incident. I thought that Mrs Sharp was trying to show that he was as disgusting and over-sexed as she had always tried to imply, but that what she found most difficult was not this side of him, but her own inability to lose her feelings about him. They both reacted furiously at this, but when their outburst had died down

128

I suggested that Mr Sharp, although he put himself over as a person who was interested in sex in a balanced and normal way, in fact betrayed his anxiety and embarrassment about it by this kind of action. There was a very tense moment at this point, but slowly this tension began to ease. Mr Sharp talked about his resentment of his wife working, and Mrs Sharp admitted that she was anxious about keeping up her duties as a wife and mother. When we had discussed these matters for a time, Mr Sharp said he supposed what I had heard and seen that day could make me a witness in a divorce case. He seemed very anxious about his outburst, both that it might turn me against him, or that I might stop visiting them. We talked about this for some time before I left.

On this occasion, Mr Sharp acted out for the first time all his angry and wild feelings towards his wife, the resentment against her which he had brought into his marriage from the start, sparked off by the half accusation of sexual inadequacy which was implied in her story about the photograph. The mask of the reasonable man slipped away altogether, and he behaved as uncontrollably as his wife had done on previous occasions. He came near to admitting his fears of his wife's growing independence, and she in turn, relieved of some of her feelings of incompetence and anger, was able to respond in a way which helped him not to deny these feelings.

From this point there was a rapid transformation in the whole family's behaviour. On my next visit, I found that Mr Sharp had completed the decorating of the house and had also tidied up the garden. Mrs Sharp remarked on a considerable improvement in David's behaviour, and her husband drew attention to the fact that he had stopped working overtime (he used to stay at work till after six o'clock) and had started to come home each evening at 4.30. There was a difficult period just before the next school holidays, when Mrs Sharp became depressed about the prospect of having to give up her job, and to cope with John, with whom she had always had the greatest difficulty. However, when I visited during the holidays I found a big difference in Mrs Sharp's relationship with John. She seemed for the first time to be enjoying his company and that of the other children. She was particularly playful with John, wrestling with him and teasing him quite skittishly. Whereas before she had plainly found the children a burden, and the only words she had spoken to them had been shouts of disapproval, she said that she found now that they were 'not too bad at times'. Mr Sharp, who had always been the one to play with the children, was sitting alone watching television, and had very little to say on this particular occasion.

I continued to visit the Sharps for another two months after this. Each time I would hold my breath, waiting for a crisis, but none came. I eventually drew attention to this, and said I felt my visits were no longer necessary. Mr and Mrs Sharp both confirmed that things were better and they were able to let me leave without producing a quarrel at the last moment.

Working with the Sharps was a dramatic, exciting experience which often had me frightened and sometimes made me very discouraged. At the time it was not easy to think clearly about what was happening, and perhaps I, like them, tended to act out my role rather than to think it out. However, in retrospect there seem to be a number of things to say about the emotional interaction which took place.

In spite of the lack of information about the family backgrounds of either Mr or Mrs Sharp, certain things about them are pretty clear. Mr Sharp, partly because of his disastrous first marriage, was a man with very great anxieties about his abilities to sustain the roles of husband and father, and in particular about his sexual role. It was very important for him to feel that he was sexually adequate, and indisputably the masculine, sexually dominant partner in the marriage. But because of his fears about himself, he could only do this by denying a number of very strong feelings. His wife, by contrast, although

130

equally unsure of her sexual identity, was more afraid of the strength of her sexual feelings than of the problems which accompanied the role of a rejecting, cold and unresponsive wife. She preferred to be seen as someone without any love or warmth for her husband than to risk the pain of being a loving wife who might be rejected by her husband. Her experience of rejection as a child had taught her to be a hard, angry person who could not be hurt, but only infuriated. She was quite prepared to see her husband as an over-sexed tyrant, to whom she could transmit all her sexual feelings, while she accepted the cold and asexual parts of his personality. These roles, however unsatisfactory, were less to be feared than the feelings which they both denied.

For Mr Sharp, the experience of his first marriage meant that he must be the one who was in control, whose wife depended on him, and could do nothing without him. He maintained this role by presenting himself as a reasonable, capable person, and his wife as unreasonable and incompetent. She, with her miserable life before marriage, had the lowest opinion of herself, and was afraid to make any real challenge to this situation because in many ways she still feared the feelings associated with the life she had had before her marriage more than the difficulties she had had since. Her opinion of herself had been so moulded by her early experiences that she could not really believe that she could be a competent and independent person; the only choice seemed to lie between her anger with her critical husband and the bitter loneliness of having nobody. She often thought of going away from him and the children, but had always turned back at the last minute out of fear of those feelings. Even as her confidence increased, she still thought in terms of leaving her family as the only alternative to putting up with the role of useless wife and incompetent mother. It was not until she had briefly tried to get away that she began to make a real attempt at becoming a more capable and independent person within her marriage. She had to face her fear of depression and conquer it before she could get a job, or even make me a cup of tea. She was thus a very willing party to Mr Sharp's family system in which he was the reasonable, dominant partner, and she easily accepted all his inadequacies and shortcomings as part of herself, while transmitting to him all the feelings which went with the often motherly role he played to John in particular.

This pattern of interaction between Mr and Mrs Sharp helped to determine the emotional roles of John and David also, and gave them their characteristic patterns of acting out. John was the one who was most like his father, and with whom his father had the closest relationship. It was he who expressed his father's wild, unreasoned resentment of Mrs Sharp, and also some of the messy, dependent part of his father's personality in his soiling. It was not until after Mr Sharp had begun to come to terms with the less reasonable side of his own feelings that John's relationship with his mother improved. After Mr Sharp had lost control and made his violent attack on his wife in front of me, not only did her capability in the house improve, but John was able to respond to her better efforts to be a mother. Once Mr Sharp took back some of his angry feelings from John, and also accepted some of his dependence on his wife in recognising his feelings about her having a job, John was able to take a very different role in the family. The close emotional link between John and his father, which Mrs Sharp had so much resented, ceased to operate as a destructive force within the family group.

David was for Mrs Sharp what John was for her husband. He expressed for her the side of her personality that, far from wanting to be left alone by her husband as she claimed, was demanding of his affection and destructively resentful of his interest in anything other than herself. David's wrecking of his father's precious equipment was the acted-out expression of Mrs Sharp's feelings about the interesting task in which her husband had been engaged early in their marriage when he had refused to have intercourse with her. Once Mrs Sharp began to recognise and

132

accept some of these feelings in herself, she transmitted less of them to David and his behaviour improved. It was noticeable that soon after admitting to stealing money from her husband (which was destined to be spent on a camera) and being able to look at some of the feelings connected with this, Mrs Sharp mentioned David's behaviour and was able to recognise something of herself in it. From this point on she began to stop complaining about the children, and to learn to play a more positive part in their lives. But it was not until after the significant scene which she made over Mr Sharp's photograph that she was sufficiently on terms with these feelings to take this role to the full extent of her powers.

Up to the time when I started visiting them again, the Sharp family could see little hope of improving their position other than in escaping from each other, and even this was blocked for them. Mrs Sharp alternated between pressing for her husband to be 'put away' and planning to leave him, while he was determined to stay put but claimed he would be quite happy if she went, simultaneously implying that it was she who needed 'treatment'. Both lacked any real help or support outside the family group and this increased their anger with each other over the state of their marriage. In a period of about a year they slowly discovered that there were emotional strengths in their relationship as well as weaknesses, and that it was safer for each of them to express his own weak and vulnerable side in the marriage than had been feared. Because of this strengthening of the emotional resources of the family, and drawing together of the parents, there was less need for the family to separate off the children and push them outside the family. A family which had seemed to do nothing but damage its members had begun to be a source of support and security for them all.

Reference

1   D. Cooper, Review of N. W. Ackerman, 'Treating the troubled family', *New Society*, 11 May 1967.

5

Working outwards from the family

While it may sometimes be realistic to think of integrative families as self-contained units with little contact with the outside world, this is certainly not true of most families, and particularly untrue of centrifugal families. For such families the network of relatives and friends with whom they have day-to-day contact is an important part of their lives.

Mayer and Timms[1] account for clients' contact with professional social workers in terms of a breakdown of the family's problem-solving methods based on this network. They quote American studies in support of this view, and their own study of sixty working-class families in which one member, usually the mother, went to the Family Welfare Association for advice or assistance. Nine out of ten of these had relatives or friends with whom they felt close. The problems they brought to the FWA were either felt to be unsuitable for this network, or else had been tried on it, but had met with an inadequate response.

To what extent does social work take account of such networks? Mayer and Timms point out that most social work literature has ignored the existence of informal resources. One approach to preventive social work might consist in trying to strengthen the resources upon which the majority of people with interpersonal problems (according to the American survey thirteen times as many as go to professional problem-solving agencies) depend. One approach to family problems which have been referred for professional help might be to aim at helping the family to re-establish methods of dealing with them within the informal network.

One of the advantages of working with families rather than individuals, and in their homes rather than our offices, is that it enables social workers to make some assessment of the kind of social and extended family network that is open to members of the family, and perhaps even to meet some of the people in them. These people are likely to be much more important to the family than a social worker ever will be.

In fields of social work other than mental health it does not take long to find that many families who are known to the agency are also known to each other. Some agencies speak of a 'problem family network'. In some areas this means that families with numerous social problems associate with each other and not with other families, perhaps initially through meetings at social work agencies. In other areas it means that the housing authorities have put several families with social problems in the same street. In still others it means that certain families living in bad conditions or on low incomes have these problems in common, and also happen to know each other.

Social workers appear often to see the existence of such networks as a threat rather than an opportunity. They feel that such 'subcultures' drag individuals down to a common low level, to instil bad habits. They fear that clients lead each other astray, compare notes about the treatment they have had from 'the Welfare', encourage each other's hostility, and hatch plots. They undo social workers' good work by keeping each other gossiping and encouraging each other to spend the money which has been prised out of official agencies on the wrong things.

Yet for all these negative qualities of such relationships, social workers are forced to recognise that they provide many of the clients with their only chance of avoiding social isolation, with a sense of group membership and solidarity, and with the reassurance that they are not alone in their situation. Furthermore, they often provide them with a certain amount of economic security through a system of lending and borrowing which only breaks down over large items like quarterly fuel bills, or accumulated rent arrears. There are times when they also provide an unofficial childminding and fostering service. Without the services provided within these relationships, the demands made by individual families on the official social work services would be very much greater.

Working with social networks

Social work's antagonism to such networks, and its anxiety about dealing with members of them, seems to be connected with its origins in providing specific services for certain individuals and families under clearly defined conditions. The bureaucratic structure of social work to which this gave rise, the necessity of limiting services to those who qualified according to statutory regulations, the importance of appearing to be just and to meet needs impartially, to treat each case on its individual merits, even the principle of confidentiality, are threatened by the fact that most clients are not individuals with individual problems, isolated from each other and quite unalike, but on the contrary are often a group of people with shared social problems (such as bad housing or low incomes) or else people who through living in close proximity with each other are well aware of the common factors in their social problems. Because social work was originally established to help such people as individuals, and to try to raise them up to an 'acceptable' pattern of behaviour, it sees others who share their difficulties as a threat, because they are likely to drag down again those who are being helped. As a result of its whole structure and traditions, social work finds it hard to recognise that people with social problems are not necessarily different from the others they associate with in day-to-day life, and may well form part of a wide group of people whose whole pattern of existence constitutes some kind of a 'social problem' in itself.

It is therefore important, with the great increase in the power to intervene in family life provided by the Mental Health Act of 1959 and the Children and Young Persons Acts of 1963 and 1969, that social work should not carry over the bureaucratic principles of earlier legislation into its work with families. The danger seems to be that many of these principles may continue to be applied under the disguise of being principles of casework, or standards of mental health. Instead of administering certain legally defined rules, the social worker imposes on people a set of alien standards of behaviour and norms of family life derived from the family patterns of the dominant social class and the mental health ideology. Families are still judged in accordance with a single inflexible standard, designed to judge their performance as an isolated unit, which fails to take account of their total social situation, and the environmental context of their lives. The help they are offered is often as a result inappropriate to their needs.

Throughout this book I have drawn attention to the importance of kinship and social networks as a very large factor in the patterns of life of many ordinary families, and especially in patterns of the centrifugal families who characteristically present certain social problems to social workers. How can social work take better account of these supportive networks which play such an important part in this pattern of family life?

Links with community work

In the case of so-called problem families, it seems that social work needs to overcome some of its fears about the demands which such networks may make on it, and to look more closely at the needs of such social groups as groups, rather than concentrating on the needs of the

137

separate individuals within them. The Seebohm Report, in its chapter on the community, states, 'the notion of a community implies the existence of a network of reciprocal social relationships which among other things ensures mutual aid and gives those who experience it a sense of well-being', and recommends 'a clear responsibility then should be placed upon the social service department for developing conditions favourable to community identity and activity'.[2] Presumably, in the case of those who are isolated from other members of the community because of their social problems, this recommendation would include the strengthening of an existing network of relationships from which people derive precisely these benefits, rather than an attempt to break it down, as in much past social work practice.

There are, of course, many problems inherent in the notion of social workers becoming involved with groups of socially disadvantaged people whose interests usually conflict with those of the more powerful members of society, and often with those of the authority by which the social worker is employed. Holman suggests that local authority social workers are unlikely to make a success of any efforts to foster social change and community development by methods which must inevitably involve some conflict between their authorities and those whom they are encouraging to participate more actively in obtaining their social rights.[3] However, Barter gives several examples of projects initiated by local authority social workers to provide services which are sufficiently flexible to meet the needs of local groups in disadvantaged areas.[4] In one of these, a worker opened a family advice centre in a deteriorated area of London, and was able to start playgroups for children which were run by the local mothers themselves, and an adventure playground, also run by parents, who managed to press the authorities to alter development plans for the area to allow its continued existence. In another, what started as a family advice centre became a focal point for 'unattached' youth, and developed into a youth club with an adjoining adventure playground. This involved allowing some of the most potentially delinquent younger members of the community a large degree of freedom in running their own activities, and in spite of some conflict with established authorities and the police, the project has survived and grown. Barter takes these projects as evidence that 'caseworkers employed in a statutory setting can successfully take part in conflict strategies designed to further social action and community development'.

On the whole, however, such ventures would tend to be seen as isolated experiments, carried out by specialists, and outside the main stream of local authority social work. This view goes back to the fears generated within the hierarchical structure of social work agencies of the consequences of having to deal with clients as groups rather than individuals, an approach to which conventional social work agencies are simply not geared. Because of the whole system of caseloads, of files, of supervision of work, and of allocation of resources, many chances of helping groups of people to act more effectively together, and to press for better conditions, go wasted, while workers seek unavailingly to lure individuals, and especially adolescents, away from groups which might more profitably be helped, as groups, to engage in more satisfying and constructive activities, or be provided with better facilities in which to interact together.

Perhaps another contributory factor to this situation is the rather vague idea that social workers tend to have about the community, and what it means to their clients. For many years before the current change of emphasis, which has restored community work to its place among the methods of social work, caseworkers tended to think of 'the community' as being something to which their clients were not adjusted, but should be. It consisted of the sort of people who found their clients' behaviour offensive, and its organisation was made up of a number of associations of respectable people, to which the client did not belong. Adjusting the client to the community thus consisted in getting him to behave in ways which were acceptable to such people, and integrating him with the community in trying to persuade him to join and take part in such associations. As a rule, clients were no more acceptable to these bodies than they were willing to take any part in them, and thus this side of the social workers' activities was often unsuccessful. Now, at last, it is coming to be recognised that clients are usually part of a social network which is their own segment of the community, and part of a loose association, without any formal organisation, which provides them with much more help and support than membership of an organised group to which they were culturally unsuited could supply. If the cohesiveness of such informal networks can be strengthened by social work help, and they can be encouraged as groups to seek ways of improving the facilities available to their members, then social workers will be doing a great deal to help the social integration of the clients within them.

In rather the same way, many social work services have been developed as providing a formal and organised way of meeting emergencies in family life which are normally met by extended family or social network facilities. Thus the Children's Act of 1948 could be seen as laying down the conditions under which children could or should be officially cared for outside their families, and the development of the child care service as providing an elaborate system whereby the children of disadvantaged or disorganised parents may be cared for by other members of the community who happen to have more advantages or be better organised. Thus, in a large city, the work of the Children's Department tends to consist of receiving children from the working-class areas into care and fostering them out in the middle-class areas. It might well be that some of this activity could be avoided if more time was spent in strengthening the informal supportive resources of those people whose children are most at risk (i.e. those who live in the most disadvantaged areas). Thus

Fitzherbert, on intensive investigation of twenty-two cases of West Indian children in care, found that in twenty of these relatives or friends existed who would have been able to provide care for the children.[5]

As a social worker employed in an agency which has no official fostering or childminding system, I have tended towards this approach in cases where families are temporarily unable to care for their children. Alternatively, where there seemed to be no appropriate resources even among the further-flung members of the family's social network, I have tended to think in terms of neighbouring clients, or friends of clients, who might be able to care for the child. Perhaps this cavalier attitude is born of neither having to deal with the very young, nor having total responsibility for the physical safety of children. However, there seems to be some validity in the notion that older children at least are likely to do better in a home which is in their own neighbourhood, which is materially similar to the one in which they have grown up, and in a family whose social and cultural patterns are similar to their own. However, the more important principle involved in this method is of working outwards from the family, trying to help it strengthen its own resources for dealing with problems, rather than providing alternative resources which are unconnected with its everyday life. If it is possible to introduce to the family a new unofficial source of help in a time of crisis, rather than provide official relief from problems, then it is less likely to come to depend on outside authorities for the solution of family difficulties.

The Fry family

Here is an example of a family with problems over one of their children in which the possibility of working outwards from the family arose. I had known Mr and Mrs Fry for two years before they started to complain of difficulties with their son, Derek, aged fourteen. Before this, they had had a very bad patch in their family life, in which Mrs Fry had been in a great deal of debt, Mr Fry had had a court appearance, and had subsequently been ill for some time, and there had been a lot of discord between them. But by this time the debts were cleared and their relationship seemed to have improved. Derek had an elder sister and two younger brothers. The brothers had done better than he at school, but Derek, who had been quiet and timid as a younger child, had given no trouble up to this time. Then all of a sudden he became moody and quick-tempered, complained that his parents treated him unfairly, and began to steal money from the home. He seemed simultaneously defiant towards his parents and very unhappy. There were frequent quarrels between him and his parents, in which they said he became uncontrollably angry, and they could not get him to see reason.

For nearly a year I visited the family, trying to help them to get on better together, with very little success. Whenever I called Mrs Fry had a string of complaints about Derek, and it was very difficult to get further than the particular incidents which had occurred since my last visit, because she was so angry with him. She compared Derek very unfavourably with his brothers, and it was obvious that he reminded her very much of his father in many of the most annoying things he did. She seemed to provoke a good deal of the conflict with him, but it was very difficult to clarify this. When I saw Derek he was sullen, silent and resentful, and clearly saw me as an instrument used by his parents against him. The situation worsened when Mr Fry started to work away from home, returning only at weekends. The relationship between Derek and his mother developed into total warfare, and she repeatedly requested that he should be removed from home. Eventually he was brought before a court and remanded for three weeks for reports. While he was away I saw Mrs Fry, who said she felt awful, both as a result of guilt and of missing Derek. She recognised that she had been hard on him, but had got to the point where she couldn't bear the sight of him. She knew it was connected with feelings about her husband, and acknowledged that she preferred to quarrel with Derek than his father at a time when he was trying to establish himself in a new job. Soon Mrs Fry was anxious to have Derek back to make a fresh start. Meanwhile, Derek was tearful and repentant, and he was allowed to return home after three weeks.

However, only a week later Mrs Fry was again complaining bitterly about him, saying he hadn't changed at all. As a result of having seen her feelings when he was away, I was able to make a braver effort at getting her to look at her own part in their difficulties, and this she was willing to do. She recognised that she was often blunt and tactless in her behaviour towards him, and that she jumped on the least thing he did and blew it up out of proportion. It was as if she regarded the things that Derek said to her in moments of petulance as if they were said by an adult who meant exactly what he was saying. She also seemed to agree that her attempt to use me to control Derek had been unsuccessful, and that it was better for me to see Derek separately at my office, and not to try to take up with him her complaints about his behaviour.

Soon after this Mrs Fry became ill, suffering from the same complaint as her husband had had earlier. She talked about how she had always had to be the strong one of the partnership, how her husband had depended on her, and how much she had resented this. She recognised a very angry and quarrelsome side of herself which had been expressed first in her relationship with her husband, and now with Derek. However, she also mentioned that her mother had had a depressive breakdown in middle age. This had started while she was still living at home, and had been the cause, she felt, of her parents separating soon after she was married, after which her mother had broken down completely, and had had to be admitted to hospital. Mrs Fry had been closer to her father than her mother, and was now much closer to her mother-in-law than her mother, on whom she said she had never depended in any way. I sensed that Mrs Fry was very much afraid of something of her mother in herself, and was fighting against the possibility of having to face this.

Mrs Fry's condition deteriorated in the following weeks, and she began to see numerous doctors and specialists about her illness. She again complained bitterly about Derek's behaviour, but was more worried about the effect it had on her. She had burst into tears on one occasion, and regarded this as a suspicious sign of 'weakness'. She was afraid of 'letting herself go' and that she might be reduced to sitting and crying. She related this without difficulty to her mother's breakdown, described it to me, and acknowledged her fear that the same would happen to her. She tried to switch to Derek's behaviour, but I focused on her difficulties, in spite of her fears about being the 'weak' member of the family. She finally acknowledged that she felt she needed help for herself, that she was really depressed, and that it was becoming a real strain on her to keep up the role of being the strong one in the family.

At this point, I felt that I was for the first time in a position to be of some help to the family. I had always suspected that it was Mrs Fry, more than any other member of the family, who needed help, for although she had the continual support of her mother-in-law and several close friends, she seemed always to be at war with one other member of the family, and this now seemed to be related to her fear of her depression, and of being like her mother. What was needed was some way of Mrs Fry accepting help in her own right, acknowledging that for once she was not the strong one, and allowing her to recognise in herself the feelings that she tended to transmit to Derek or her husband. After discussing this with Mrs Fry and her doctor, I referred her to the Mental Health Service, whose social worker visited her and offered her a place in a weekly group, consisting partly of former in-patients and partly of people like herself who had never had any form of psychiatric treatment. Mrs Fry found this offer very acceptable, and said that she would be pleased to attend the group.

However, though her state of mind seemed to improve from this moment, her complaints about Derek redoubled. It was as if she was making one last attempt to put her difficulties outside herself, and through Derek, outside the family. The first problem was that she insisted that because of Derek's impossible behaviour in the home, she could not attend the group. Thus her insistence that Derek was the real difficulty became an effective means of her avoiding actually having to take what she herself had acknowledged to be a step towards an improvement in her situation.

On the other hand, the difficulty over Derek was real enough. His behaviour at home had got worse again, and he tended to quarrel with his sister and brothers. At this time, Derek had become friendly with Norman Horn (see chapters 2 and 3) who lived on the same estate. Derek spent quite a lot of time with the Horn family, who liked him, and welcomed him in their home, and it seemed that Derek found it easier to get on with the Horns than his own family at this time. Mrs Fry knew the Horns slightly and was faintly disapproving about Derek's relationship with Norman. However, when I suggested that Derek might spend the evening with the Horns when she went to the group, Mrs Fry agreed quite readily to this, and encouraged me to make the arrangements, which I did.

When I next saw Mrs Fry there had been a big improvement in her health, and she looked much less worn-out and depressed. However, she had just as many complaints about Derek. After she had talked of these for a long time, and it was plain that their relationship was as bad as at any time, I said I felt pretty certain that if it had not been for the experience of how she had felt when he was in the remand home, she would have been suggesting that Derek should be taken away from home. We discussed this, and she said that she knew not only that she would miss him, but also that it wouldn't do him any good. She said she felt very guilty about the fact that they were so bad for each other, but she couldn't help feeling angry and rejecting towards him. There were times when she felt she would be much better off if he left home, and told him so, and there were times when she felt like leaving herself. I said I realised that it must seem very unfair to her that there was nowhere for Derek to go officially which would help both her and him, but I thought it best to recognise the fact that the statutory provisions were pretty rigid, and not really the answer to the sort of problem that she and Derek had with each other. We were able to agree that return to court and removal of Derek from home, with loss of parental rights on her part, was something she very definitely did not want. She then went on to look at other possibilities of herself and Derek getting some relief from each other, and we agreed that these seemed to rest on the hope of finding someone locally to whom Derek would be willing to go voluntarily, but from whom he could return quite easily to his family whenever both could agree to this. I felt fairly sure that Mrs Fry knew that it was in my mind at this point to suggest that Derek might stay with Norman Horn's family for a time. However, I did not actually say this and Mrs Fry went through all her friends and relatives in turn, giving the reasons why it was impossible for them to have him. Finally, she thought of her mother, who was retiring from work in a few months' time, and realised that it would be possible for her to have Derek. After giving some thought to this, she realised that it might be quite a good short-term solution to the difficulties she was having with him. She became quite positive about the idea, and was cheerful by the time I left.

From this point onwards there was a steady improvement in the relationship between Mrs Fry and Derek. In the end she neither attended the group nor asked her mother to have Derek to stay. However, in discussing these matters with her, I think I was able to show her that at the same time as trying to help her develop her own resources for dealing with the difficulties in her family, including helping her to face up to the feelings about family life which she most dreaded in herself, I was also interested in assisting her to find ways of getting more effective support from outside the family during a specially difficult time with Derek. Because Mrs Fry did have a network of friends and relatives to whom she habitually turned for help in similar matters, she could readily accept this kind of approach, even if in the end she was able to manage without it.

This is just one small example of the kind of opportunity that may arise, in the process of working with families, for shifting the focus of work to the wider social context outside the nuclear family group in an effort to strengthen the family's resources, rather than provide official means of separating off its difficult members. It is in this kind of approach to helping families that some links are made between family work and group and community work, through working outwards from the family.

There are, of course, difficulties about encouraging people with social problems to associate with each other. Even in this example, the friendship between Derek Fry and Norman Horn met with some outside disapproval. Because they were the only two boys in their immediate neighbourhood who had been in trouble recently, it was easy for people to see their association as a threat. Derek's headmaster rang me up on one occasion when he had missed a day's school to say that he was sure that Norman (who attended a different school) was responsible for Derek's absence. Although Derek had been to Norman's house on the day in question, this was not at all the case, and I had not only to make the position clear to the headmaster, but also to warn Derek later about jeopardising his friendship by missing school in a way which led Norman to be blamed. However, since then Norman and

Derek have begun attending a youth club together several evenings a week, which has both improved their social life and eased the tension in their families, so in the long run I have not had cause to regret my active encouragement of their friendship.

The social worker's fear about encouraging all kinds of associations between people with social problems is in many ways similar to the fear about turning people who are trying to escape from family problems back towards the family group. There is always the fear that people whose resources are small and who are painfully aware of their own difficulties will damage each other rather than help each other, so it seems much safer to collude with those who want to get away from a 'bad' family or a 'bad' neighbourhood. But just as real family work is concerned with helping people to deal with the shared difficulties in their lives, so much group and community work can usefully start by getting people to look at how they can help each other with the problems they have in common. Thus the trend towards increased interest in forming supportive groups for disadvantaged people, and working with neighbourhoods as well as individuals, is not out of keeping with the practice of family casework. This fact is all the more apparent where family patterns in a neighbourhood reflect strong ties between neighbours who form part of a social network. There is thus a real need for social workers to be interested in the family not as an isolated unit but as part of a wider social system.

Heraud points out that caseworkers tend to see most problems in the family in psychodynamic terms.[6] However, Seebohm's recommendations,[7] emphasising the family in the community, demand a rethinking of their approach to such problems: 'A sociological approach to the family appears one of the most promising aids to this process'. Such an approach should be seen not as an alternative, but as an essential part of the understanding of the family. For, as I have suggested throughout this book, unless we see the family in its social context any analysis we make

148

of its emotional dynamics can only be misleading and incomplete.

References

1　J. E. Mayer and N. Timms, *The Client Speaks: Working Class Impressions of Casework*, Routledge & Kegan Paul, 1970.

2　*Report of the Committee on Local Authority and Allied Personal Social Services*. Cmnd 3703. HMSO, 1968.

3　R. Holman (ed), *Socially Deprived Families in Britain*, Bedford Square Press, 1970; and 'The wrong poverty programme', *New Society*, March 1969.

4　J. Barter, 'Community work by statutory authorities', in *Report of the Study Group on the Meaning and Implications of Community Care*, United Nations, 1969.

5　K. Fitzherbert, *The West Indian Child in London*. Occasional Papers in Social Administration, Bell, 1967.

6　B. J. Heraud, *Sociology and Social Work*, Pergamon Press, 1970.

7　Seebohm Report, op. cit.

Further reading

Family communication and interaction

ACKERMAN, N. W., *The Psychodynamics of Family Life*, Basic Books, 1958.

ACKERMAN, N. W., 'Family psychotherapy and psychoanalysis: the implications of difference', *Family Process*, 1, 30-43, 1962.

ACKERMAN, N. W., *Treating the Troubled Family*, Basic Books, 1966.

BATESON, G., 'Minimal requirements for a theory of schizophrenia', *Archives of General Psychiatry*, 2, 477, 491, 1960.

BELL, N. W. and VOGEL, E. F. (ed), *The Family*, Free Press, 1960.

JACKSON, D. D. (ed), *The Etiology of Schizophrenia*, Basic Books, 1960.

LAING, R. D., *Intervening in Social Situations*, Association of Family Caseworkers, 1969.

LIDZ, T., 'Schizophrenia and the family', *Psychiatry*, 21, 21-7, 1958.

LOMAS, P. (ed), *The Predicament of the Family*, Hogarth Press, 1967.

PEASE, M., 'Is the double bind a myth?', *New Society*, 24 September 1970.

RYCKOFF, I. M., DAY, J. and WYNNE, L. C., 'Maintenance of stereotyped roles in families of schizophrenics', *Archives of General Psychiatry*, 1, 93-8, 1959.

SPECK, R. V., 'Psychotherapy of the social network of a schizophrenic family', *Family Process*, 6, 2, 1967.

Sociological studies of the family

GOODE, W. J., *The Family*, Prentice-Hall, 1964.

HARRIS, C., *The Family*, Allen & Unwin, 1969.

KERR, M., *The People of Ship Street*, Routledge & Kegan Paul, 1958.

KLEIN, J., *Samples from English Cultures*, Routledge & Kegan Paul, 1965.

LITWAK, E., 'Occupational mobility and extended family cohesion,' *American Sociological Review*, 25, 1960.

LITWAK, E., 'Geographical mobility and extended family cohesion', *American Sociological Review*, 26, 1961.

MOGEY, J., *Family and Neighbourhood*, Oxford University Press, 1956.

PARSONS, T. and BALES, R., *Family Socialisation and Interaction Process*, Routledge & Kegan Paul, 1956.

ROSSER, C. and HARRIS, C., *The Family and Social Change*, Routledge & Kegan Paul, 1965.

WILLMOTT, P. and YOUNG, M., *Family and Class in a London Suburb*, Routledge & Kegan Paul, 1960.

Social work and the family

GOLDBERG, E. M., 'The normal family—myth and reality', in Younghusband, E. (ed), *Social Work with Families*, Allen & Unwin, 1965.

HERAUD, B., *Sociology and Social Work: Perspectives and Problems*, Pergamon, 1970.

LEONARD, P., *Sociology in Social Work*, Routledge & Kegan Paul, 1966.

MAYER, J. E. and ROSENBLATT, A., 'The client's social context: its effect on continuance in treatment', *Social Casework*, 45, 511-718, 1964.

MAYER, J. E. and ROSENBLATT, A., 'Client disengagement and alternative treatment resources', *Social Casework*, 47, 3-12, 1966.

PARKINSON, G., 'Marriages on probation', *New Society*, 22 May 1969.

PARKINSON, G., 'I give them money', *New Society*, 5 February 1970.

TIMMS, N., *A Sociological Approach to Social Problems*, Routledge & Kegan Paul, 1967.

YOUNGHUSBAND, E. (ed), *Social Work with Families*, Allen & Unwin, 1965.